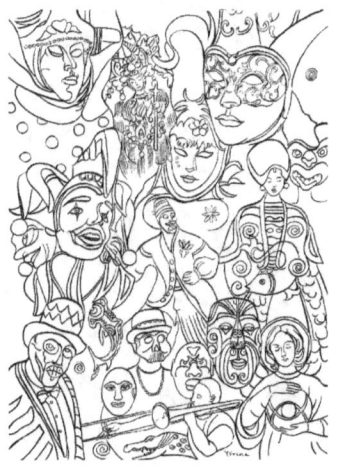 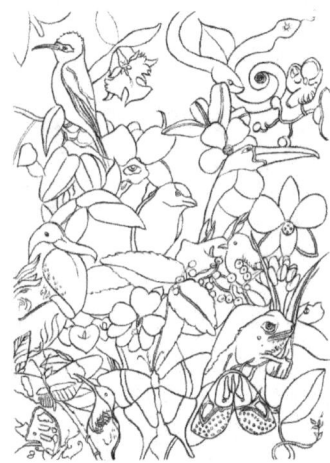 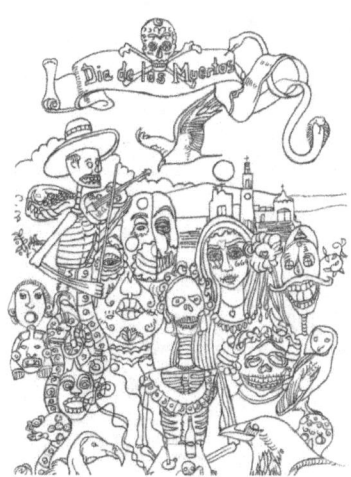

LEGENDS & TRADITIONS is an original colouring book reflecting mor3e than illustrations. Each image is based on different influences of art, cultural events, legends, traditions or nature around the world.

Appealing all ages, experience the phenomenon of colouring, enjoy the calm and let your imagination get deep in the wonderful world of colours.

LEGENDS & TRADITIONS is mirror reflecting different cultures around the world. In it you will find images of ancestral art, traditions and legends that have been passed down to us.

Enjoy the beauty of our heritage. John.

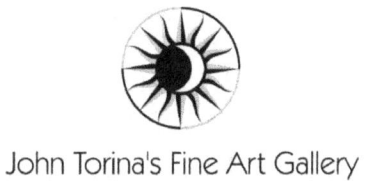

John Torina's Fine Art Gallery

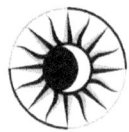

John Torina's Fine Art Gallery

Published in 2016 by John Torina's Fine Art Gallery
©2016 Copyright by John Torina's Fine Art Gallery.
®All rights reserved. First Edition.

John Torina's Fine Art Gallery
P.O.Box.: 1287-1250
Escazú, San José, Costa Rica
Phone: +506 7017-1775
Email: info@johntorina.com
www.JohnTorina.com

First printing: March, 2016
Translation to Spanish: Carmen M. Baltodano Q.
ISBN10-13: 1522962166 / 9781522962168
Special prices for schools and other institutions.

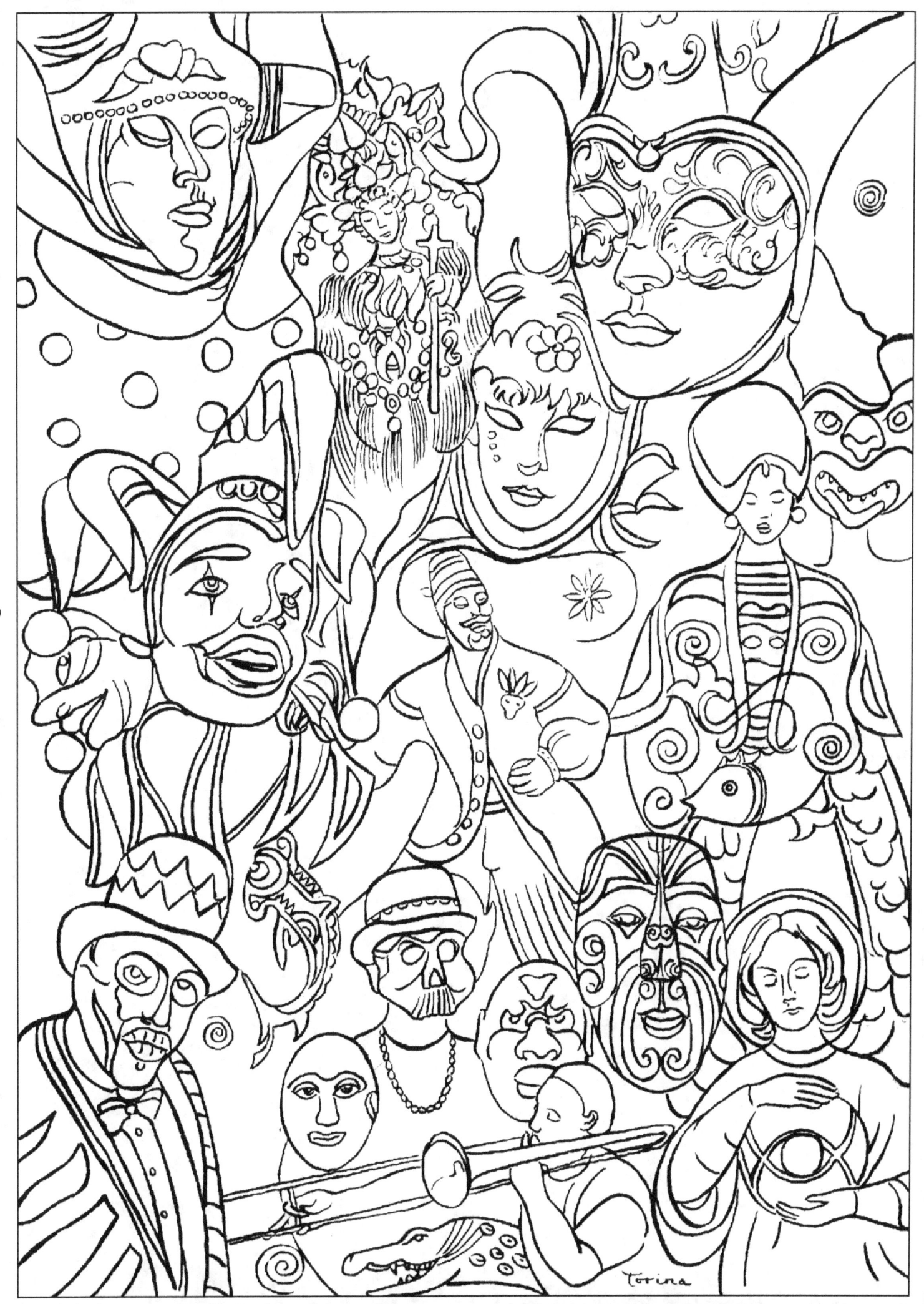

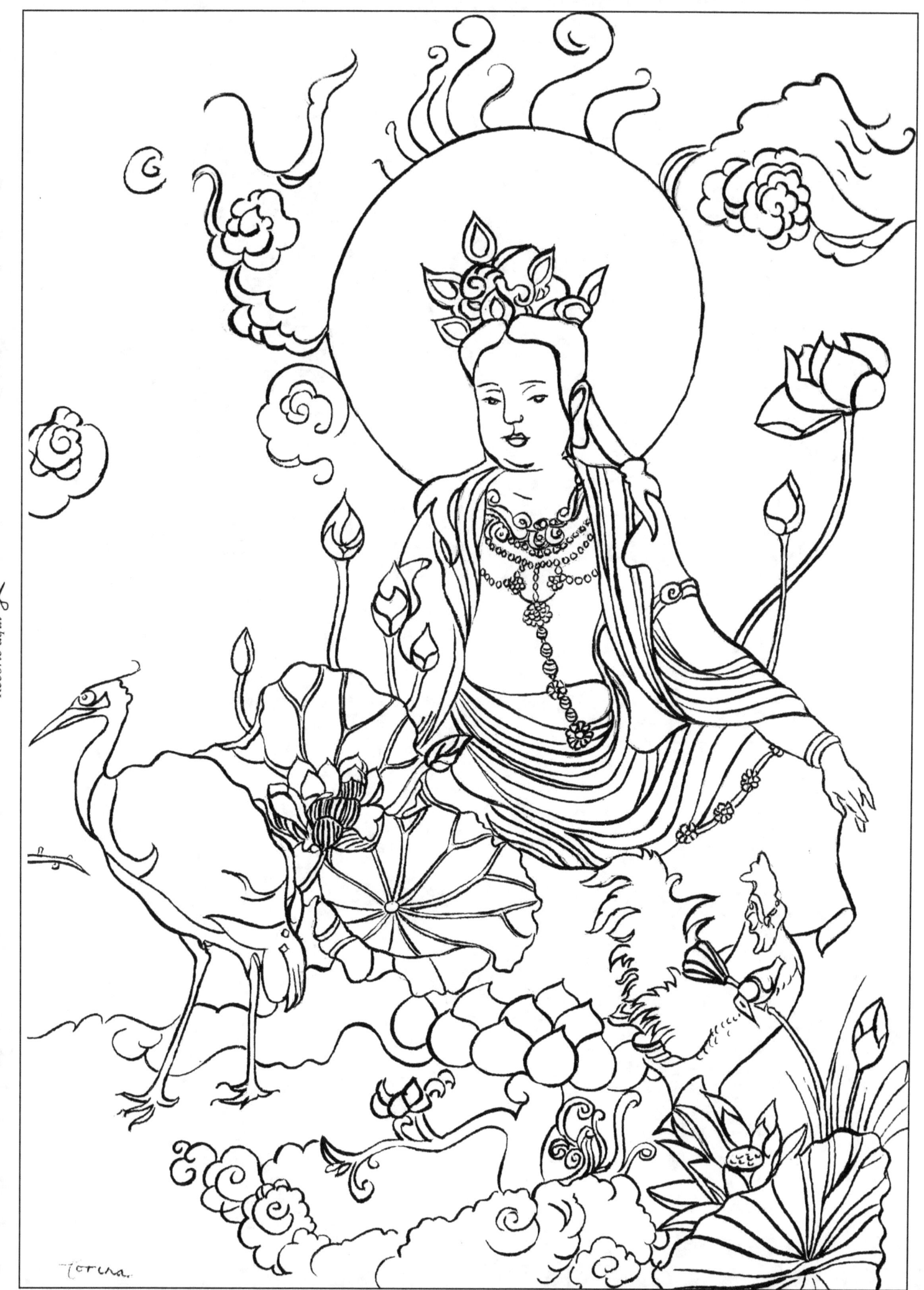

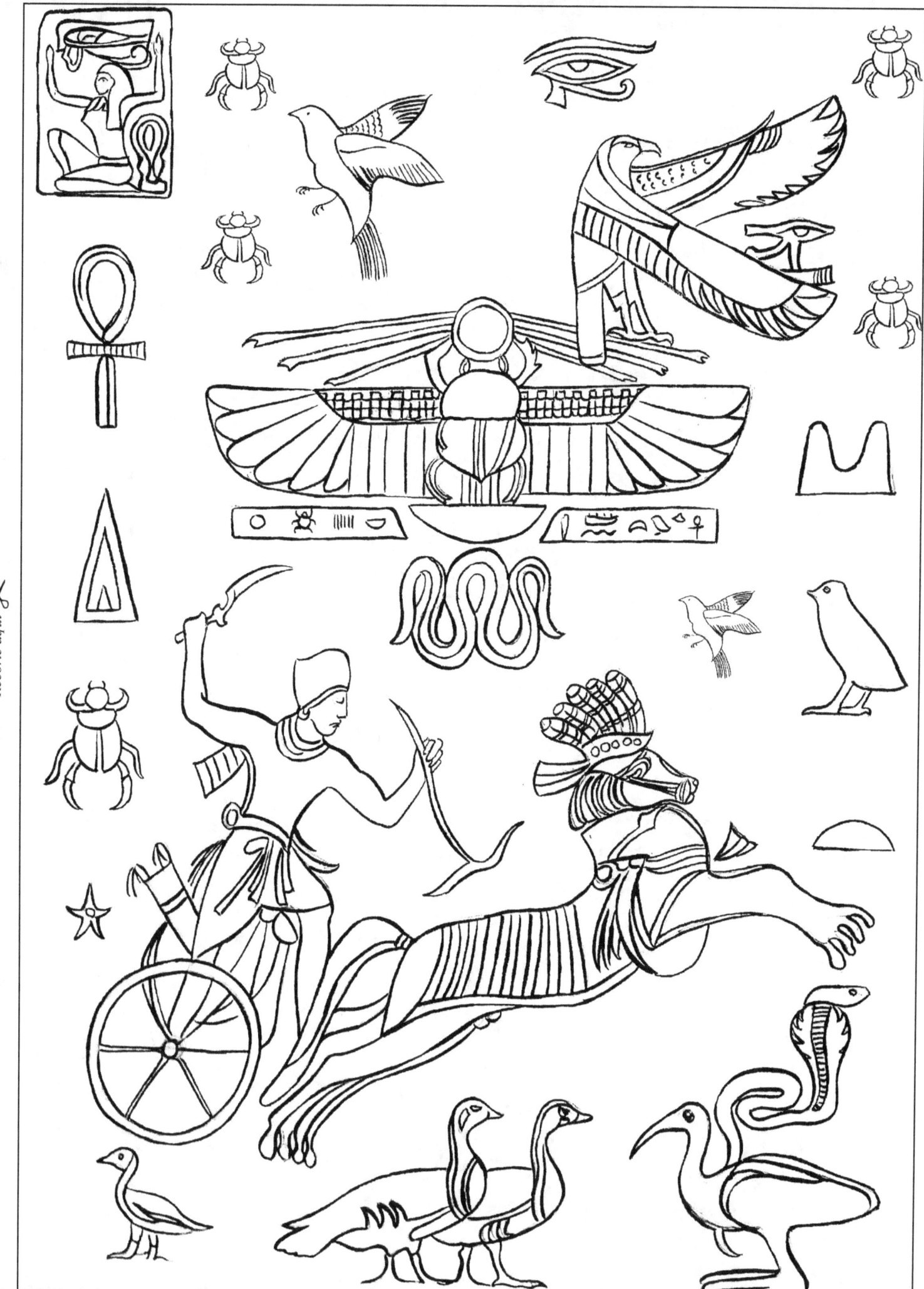

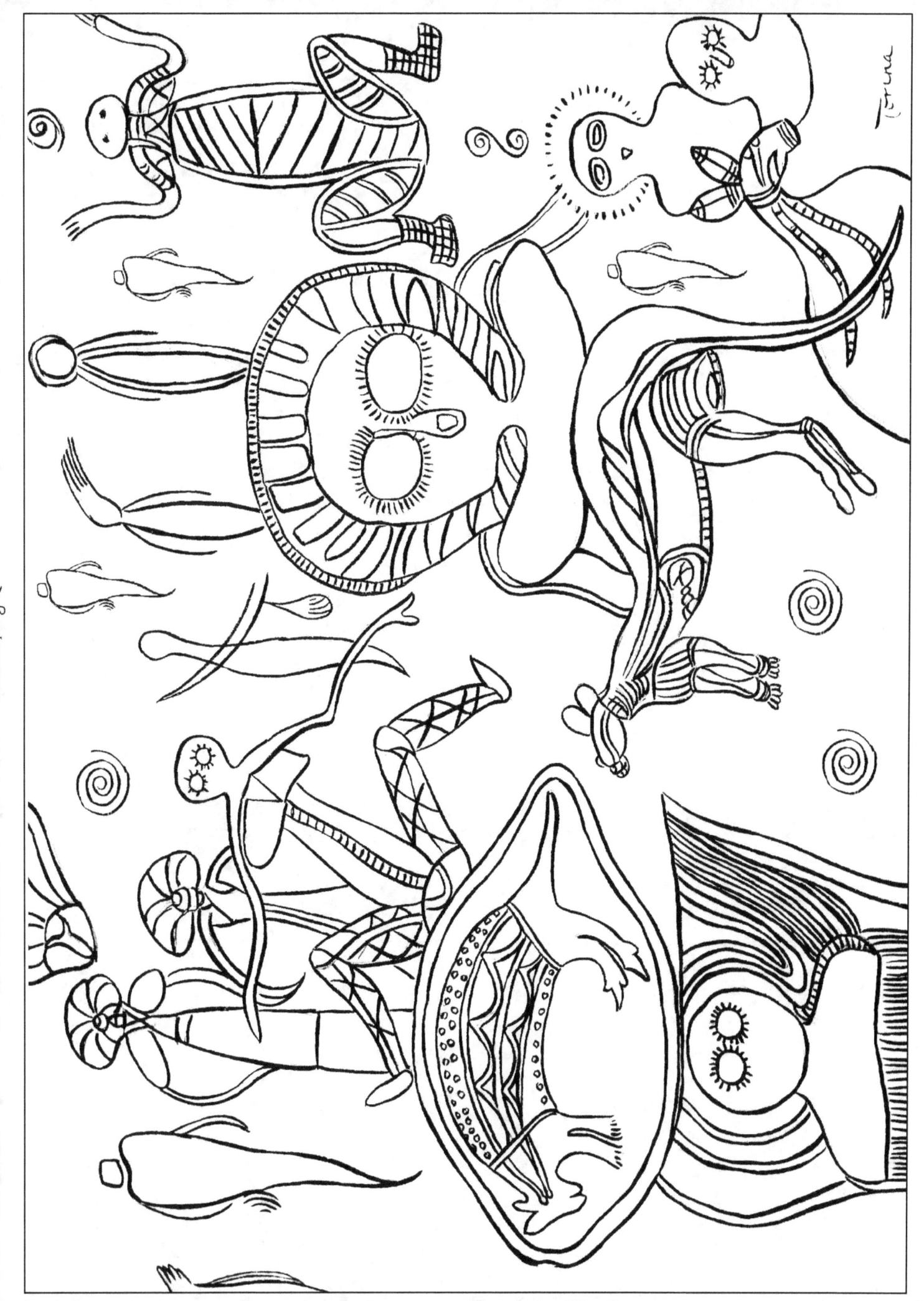

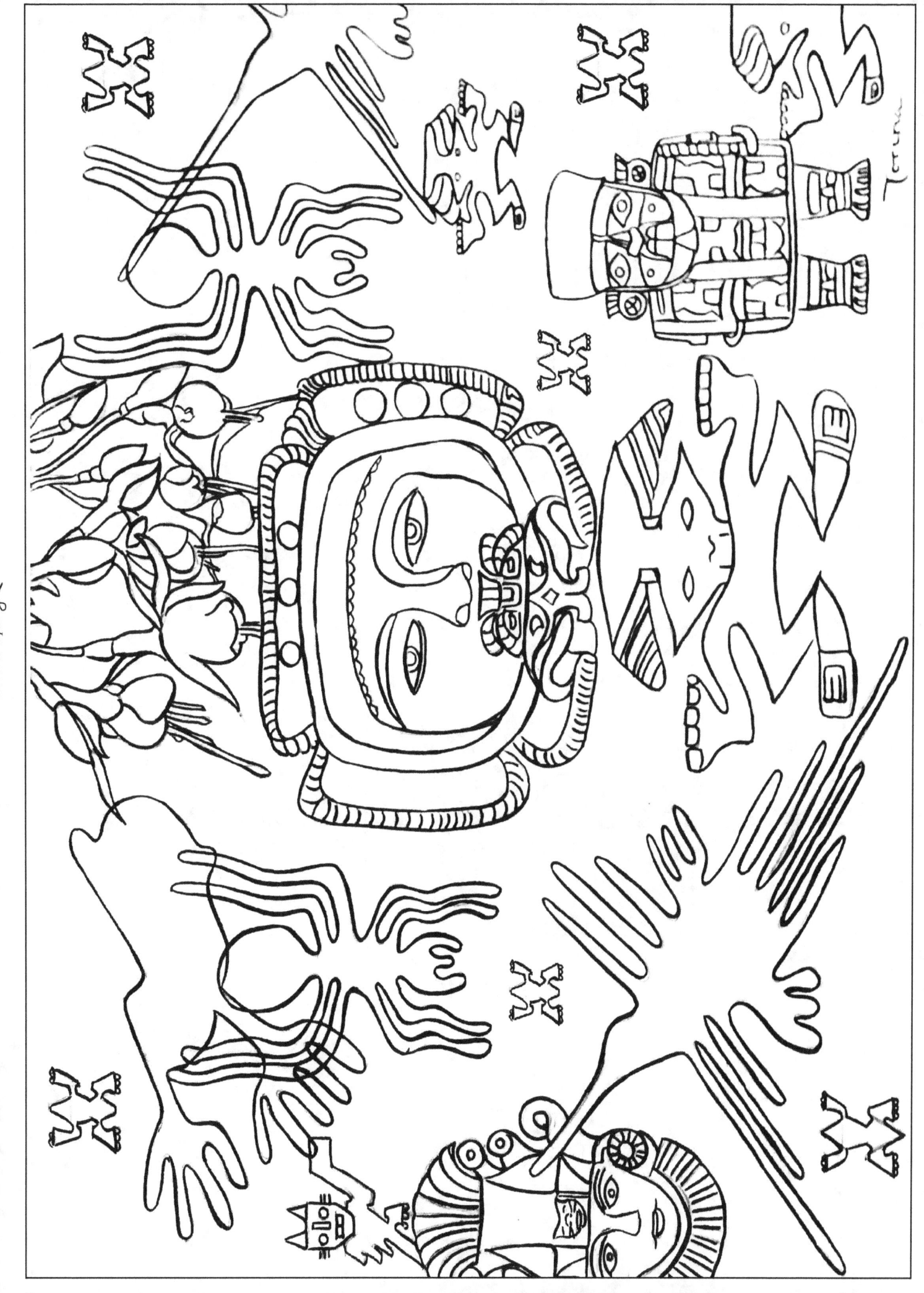

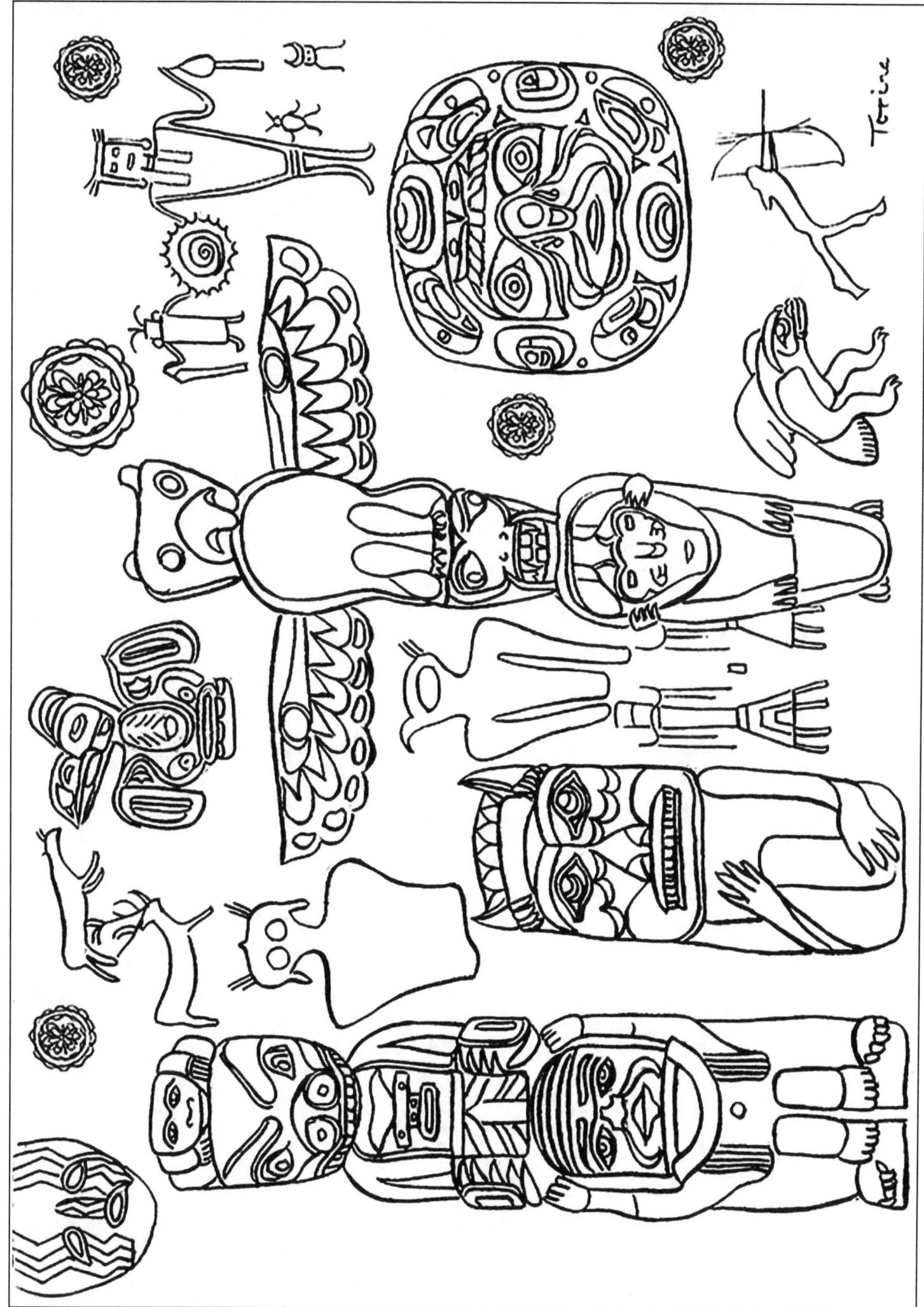

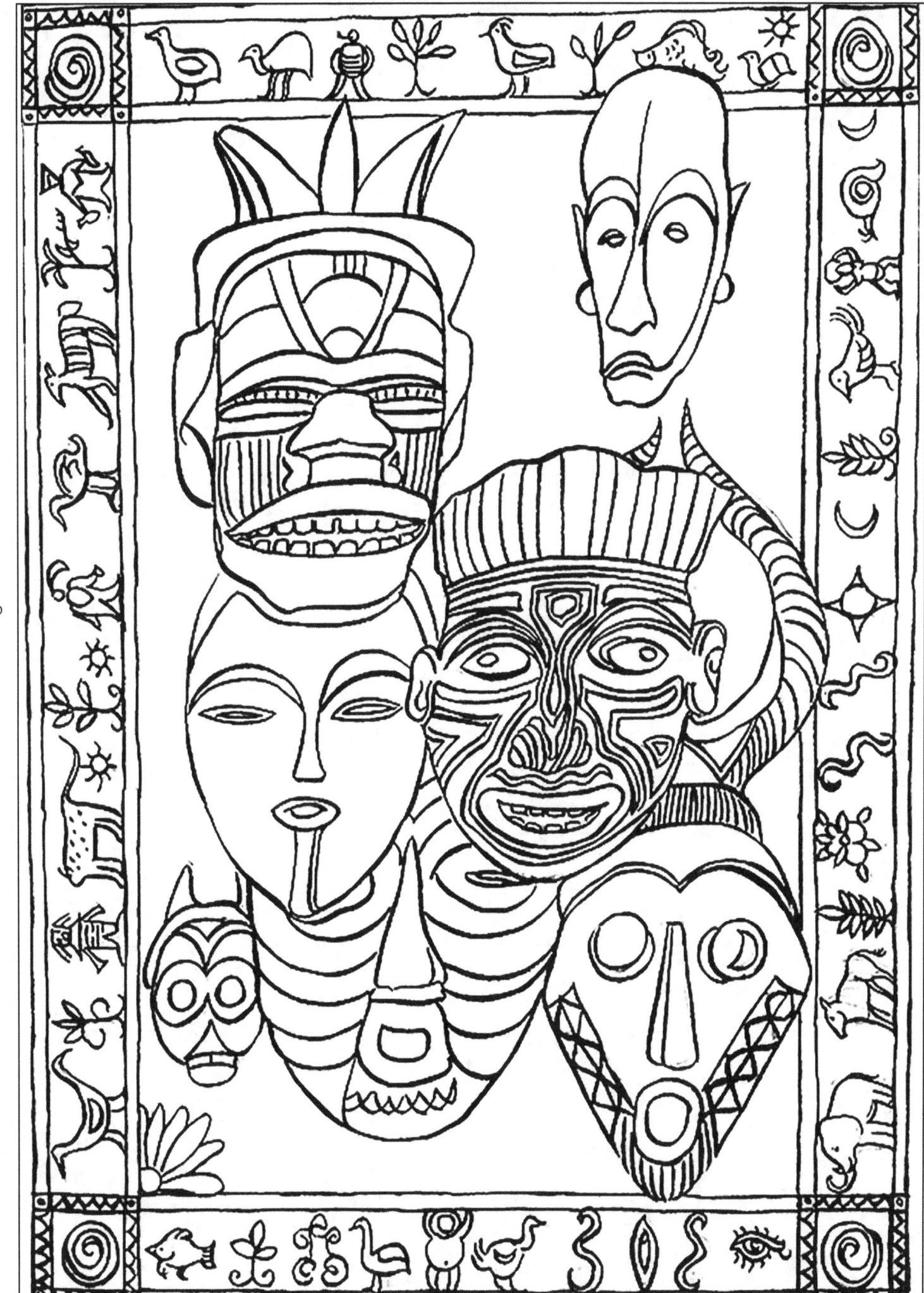

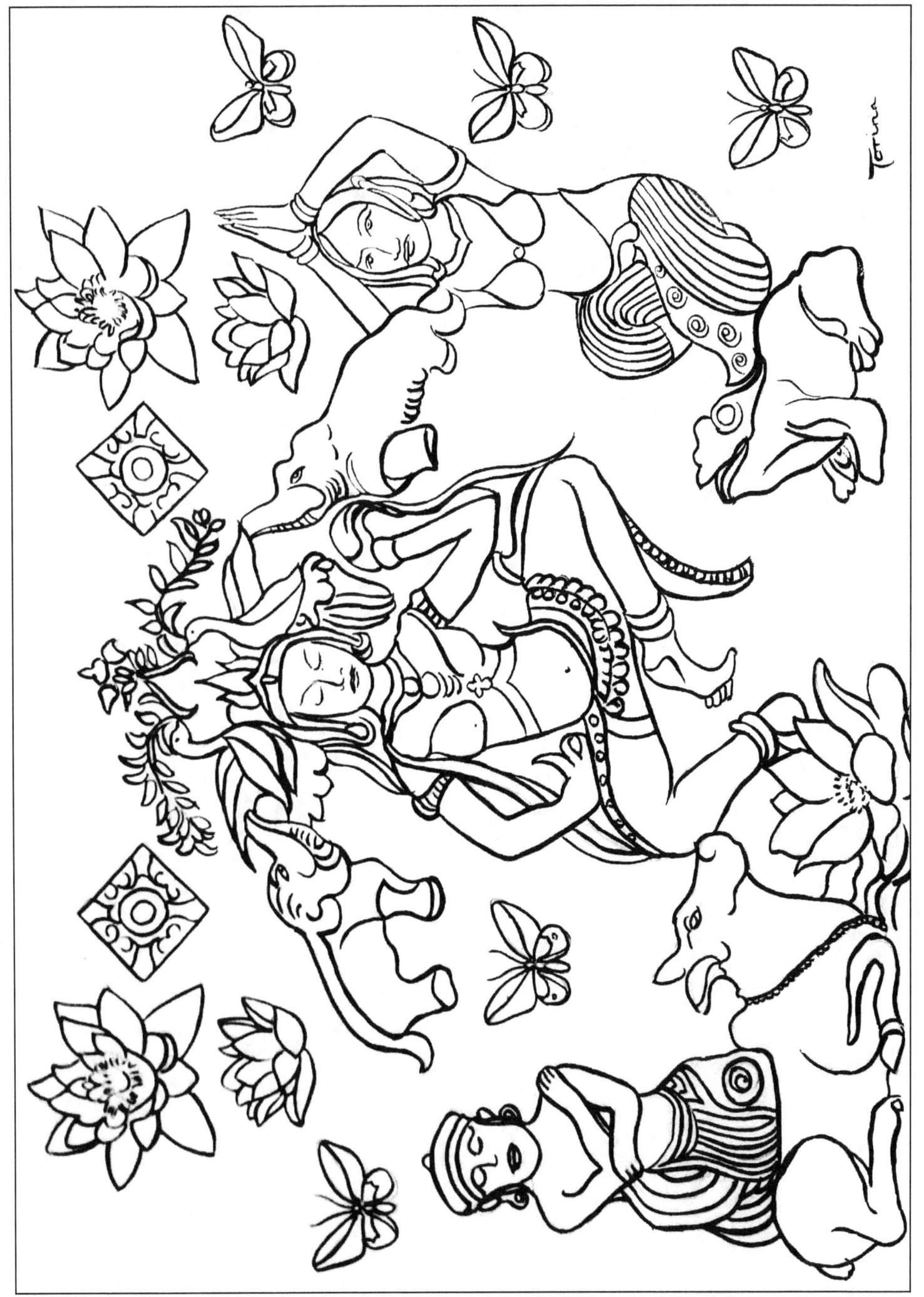

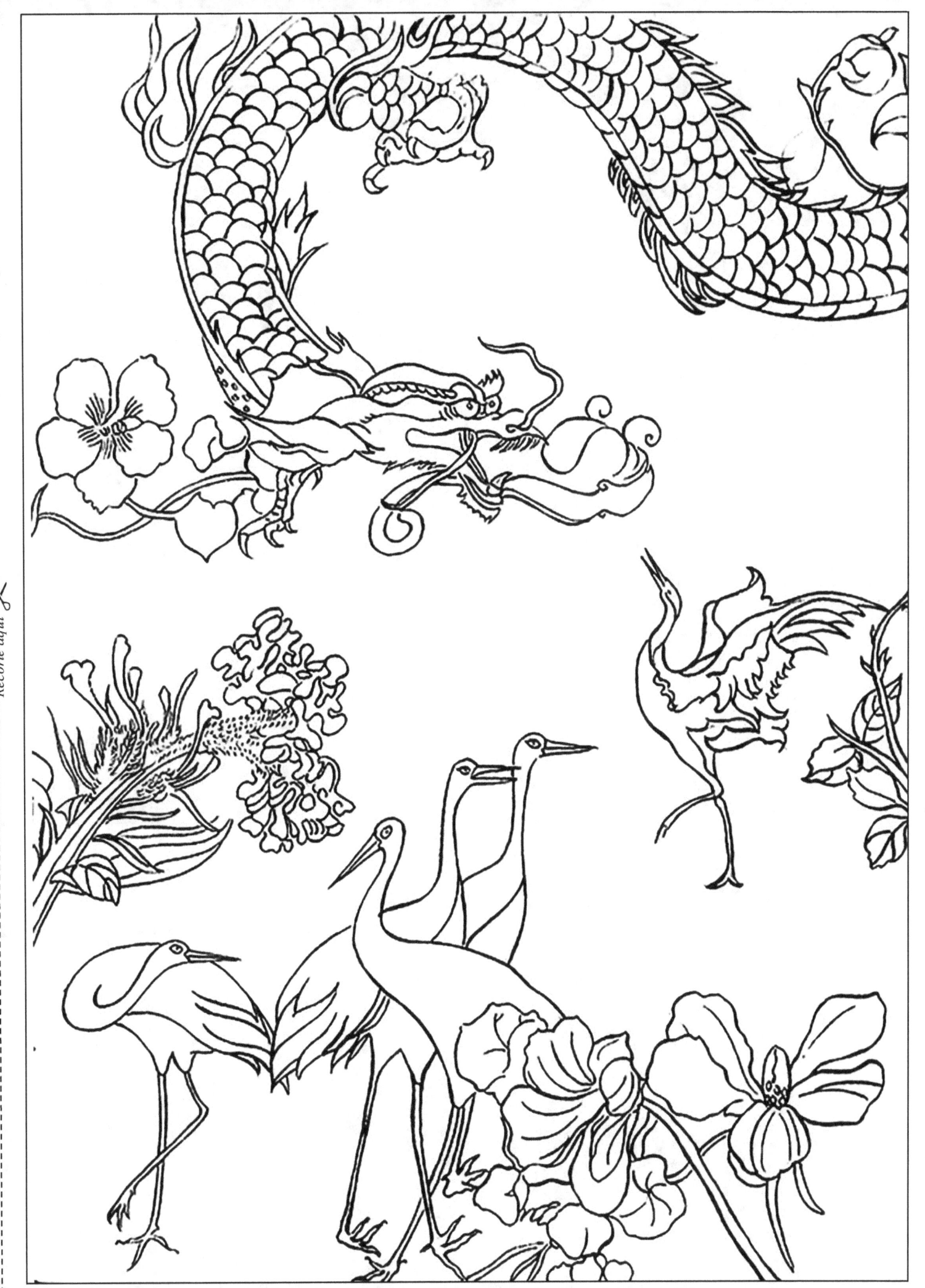

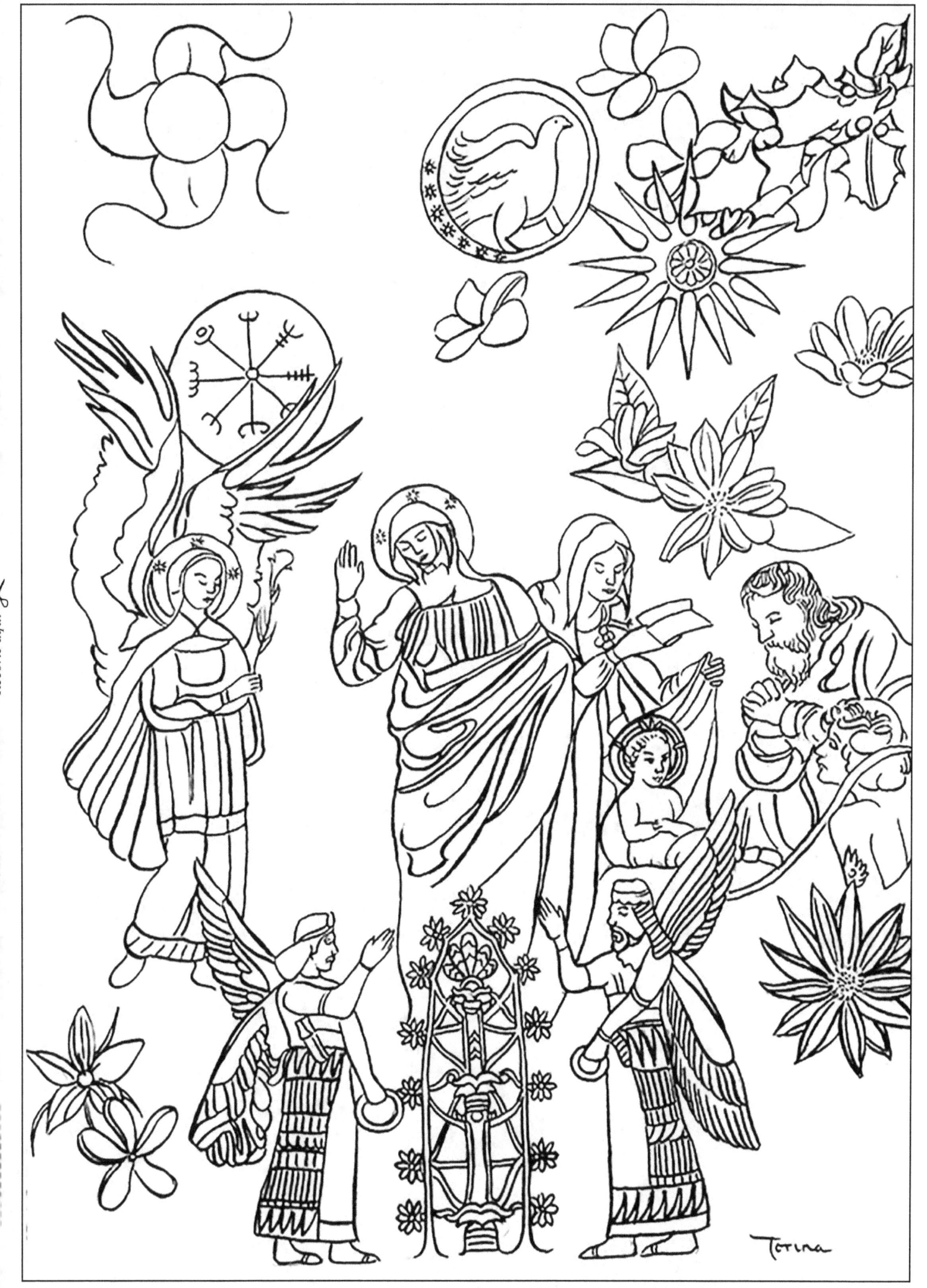

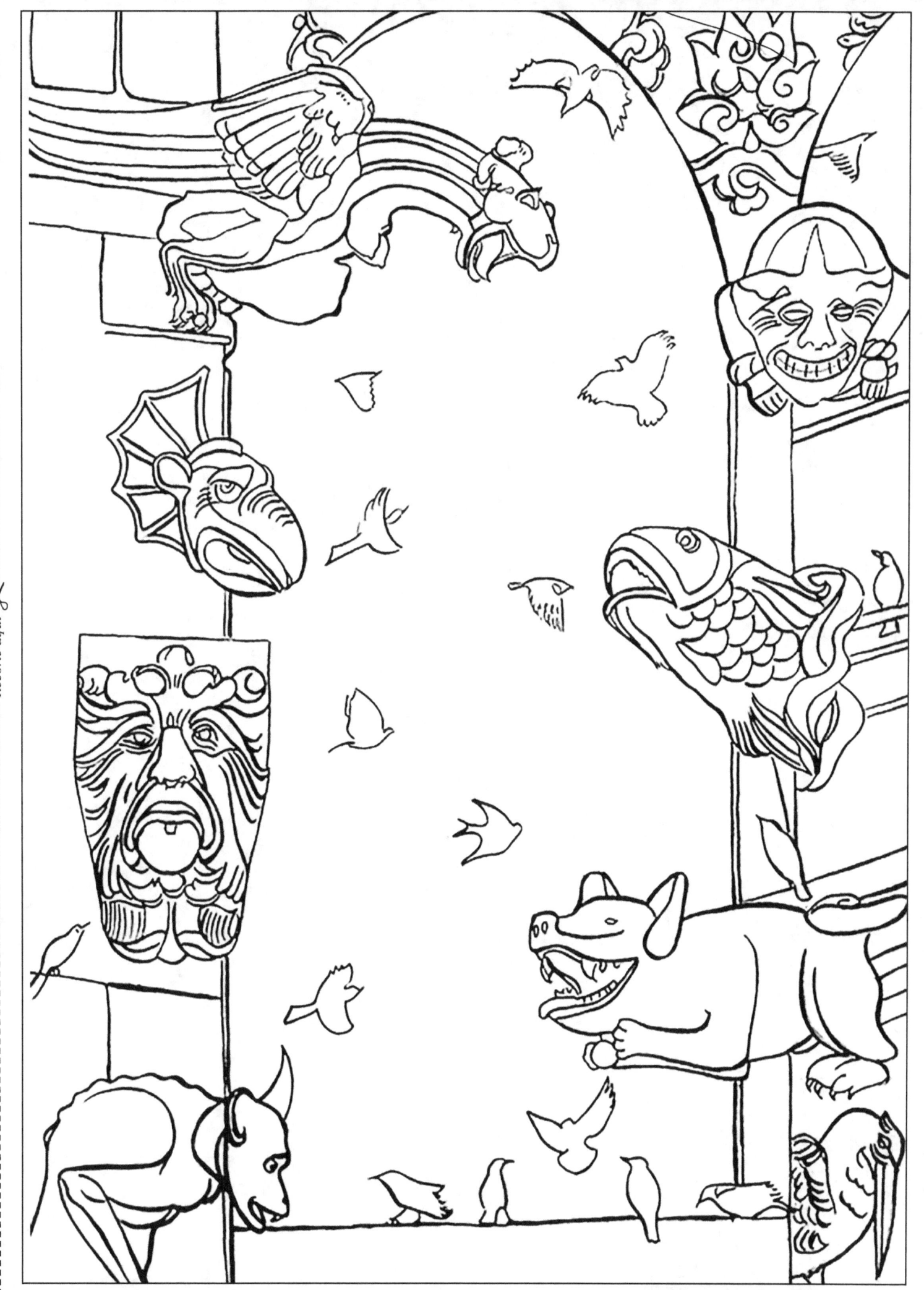

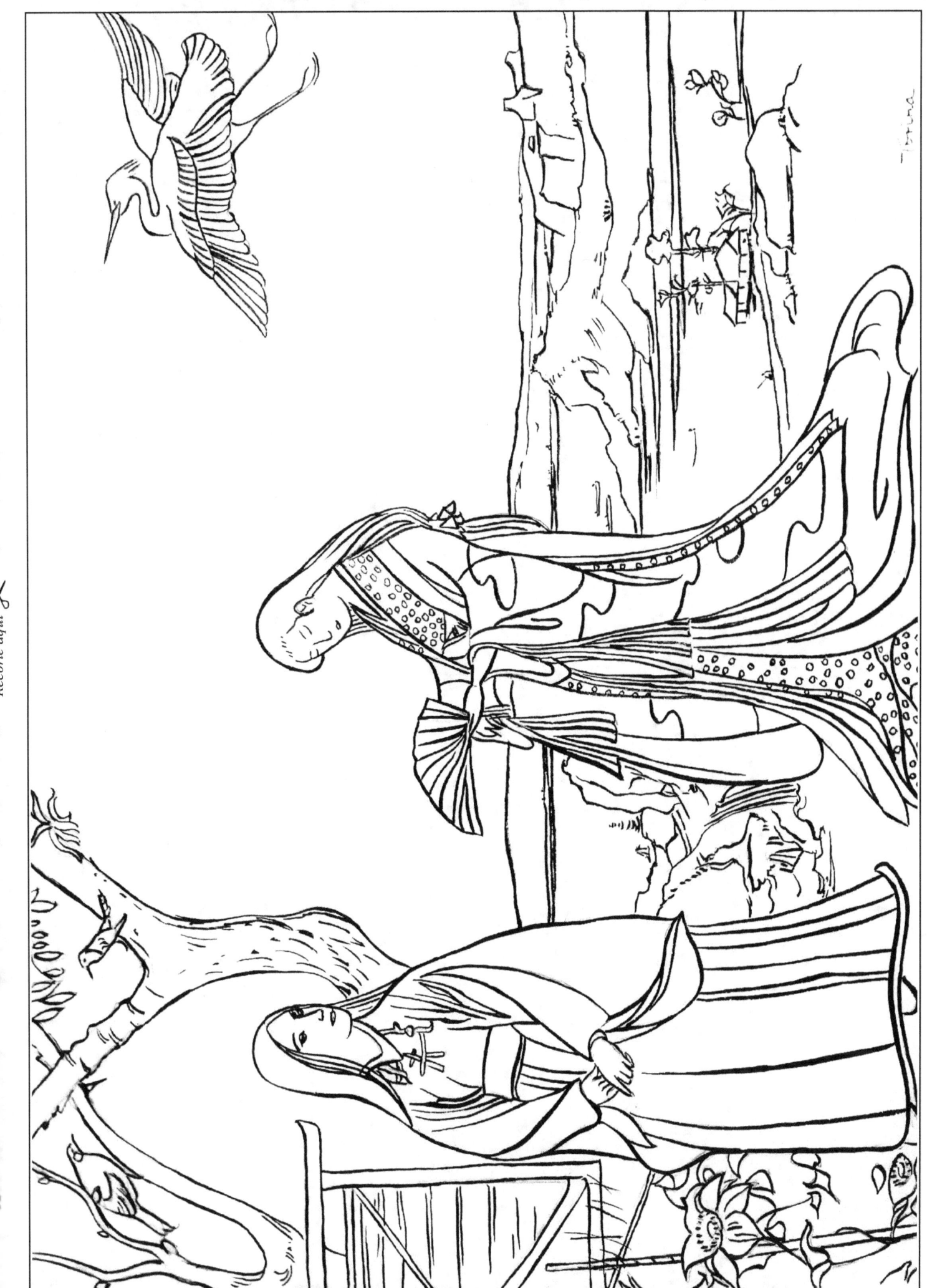

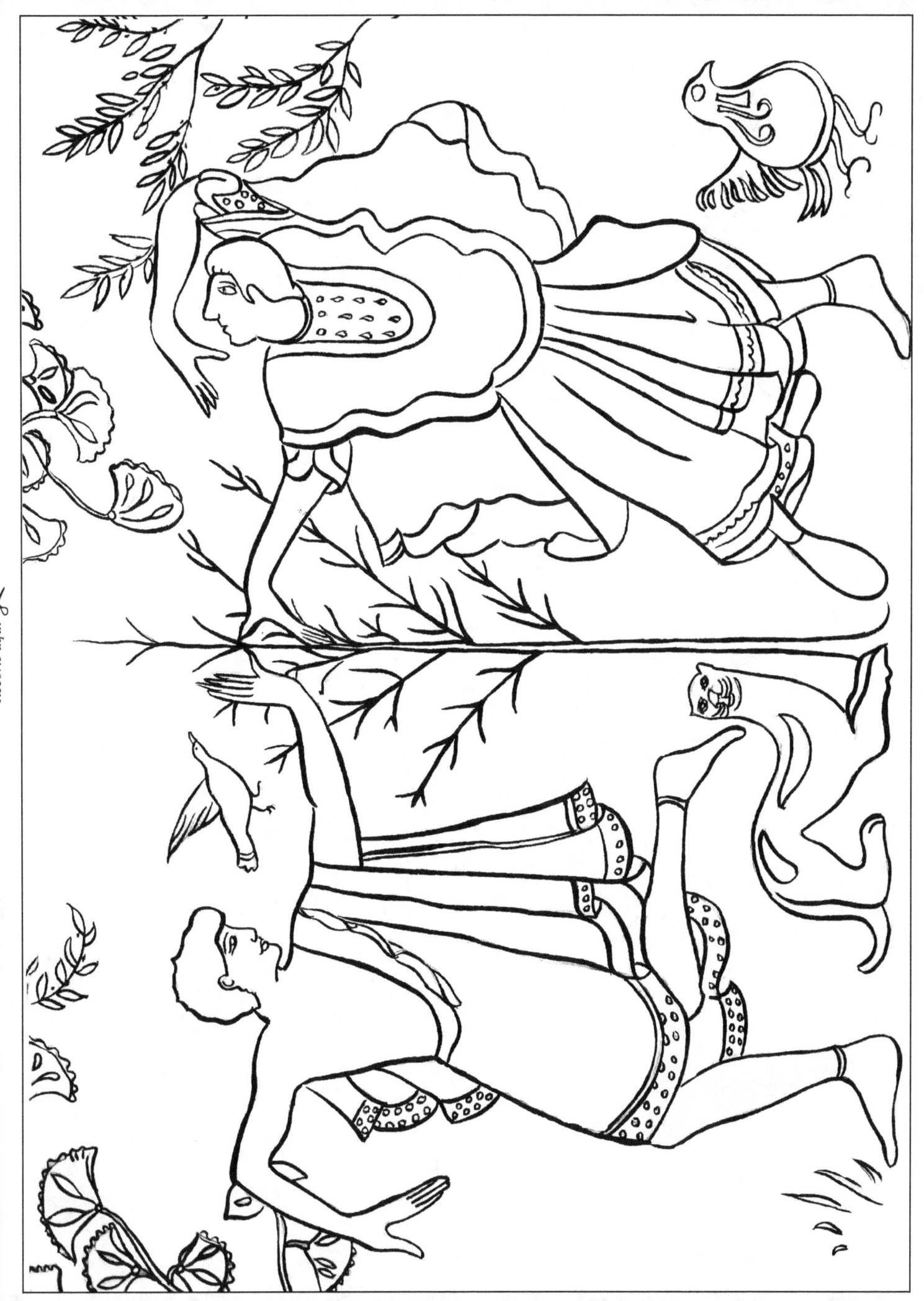

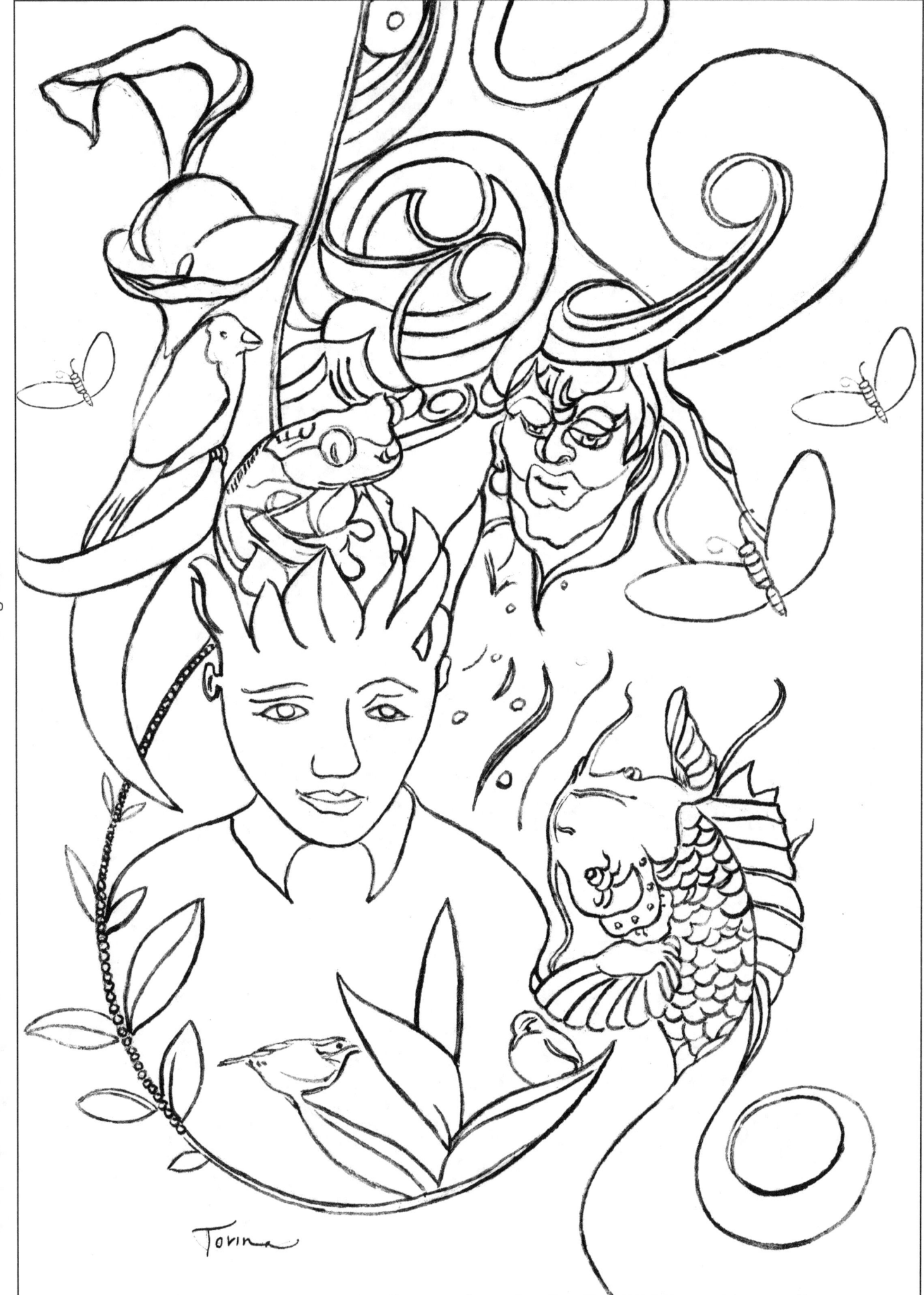

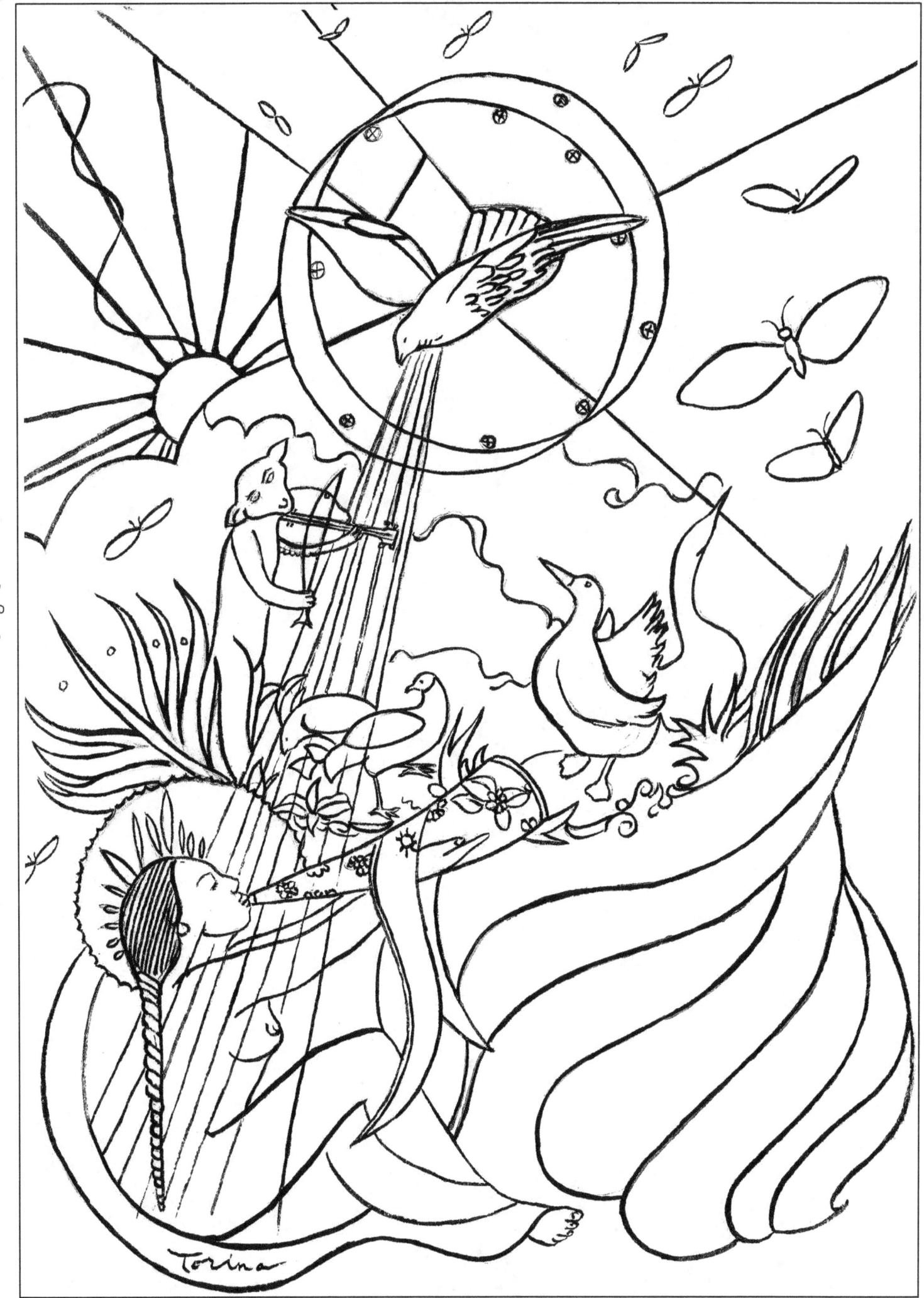

Torina

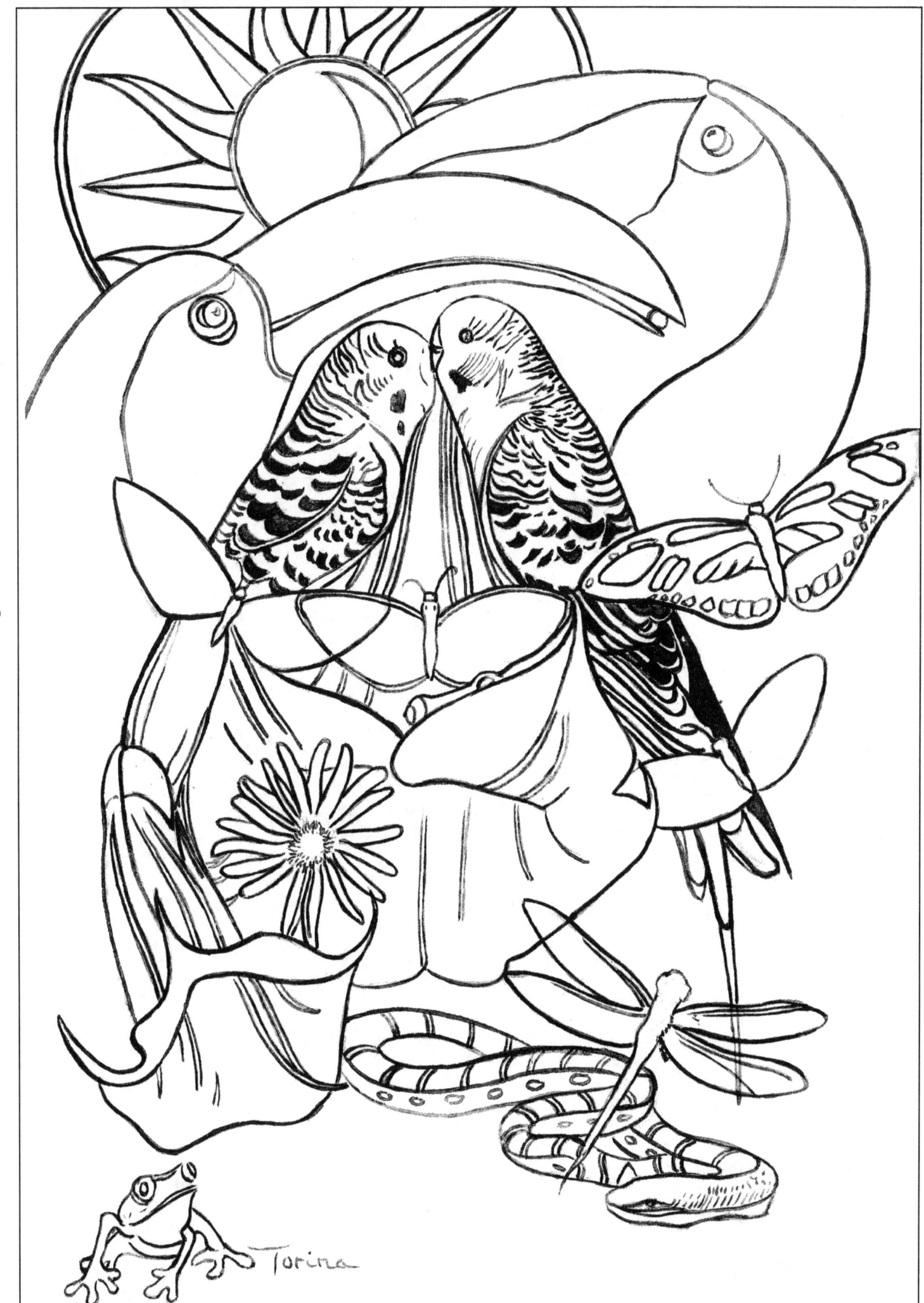

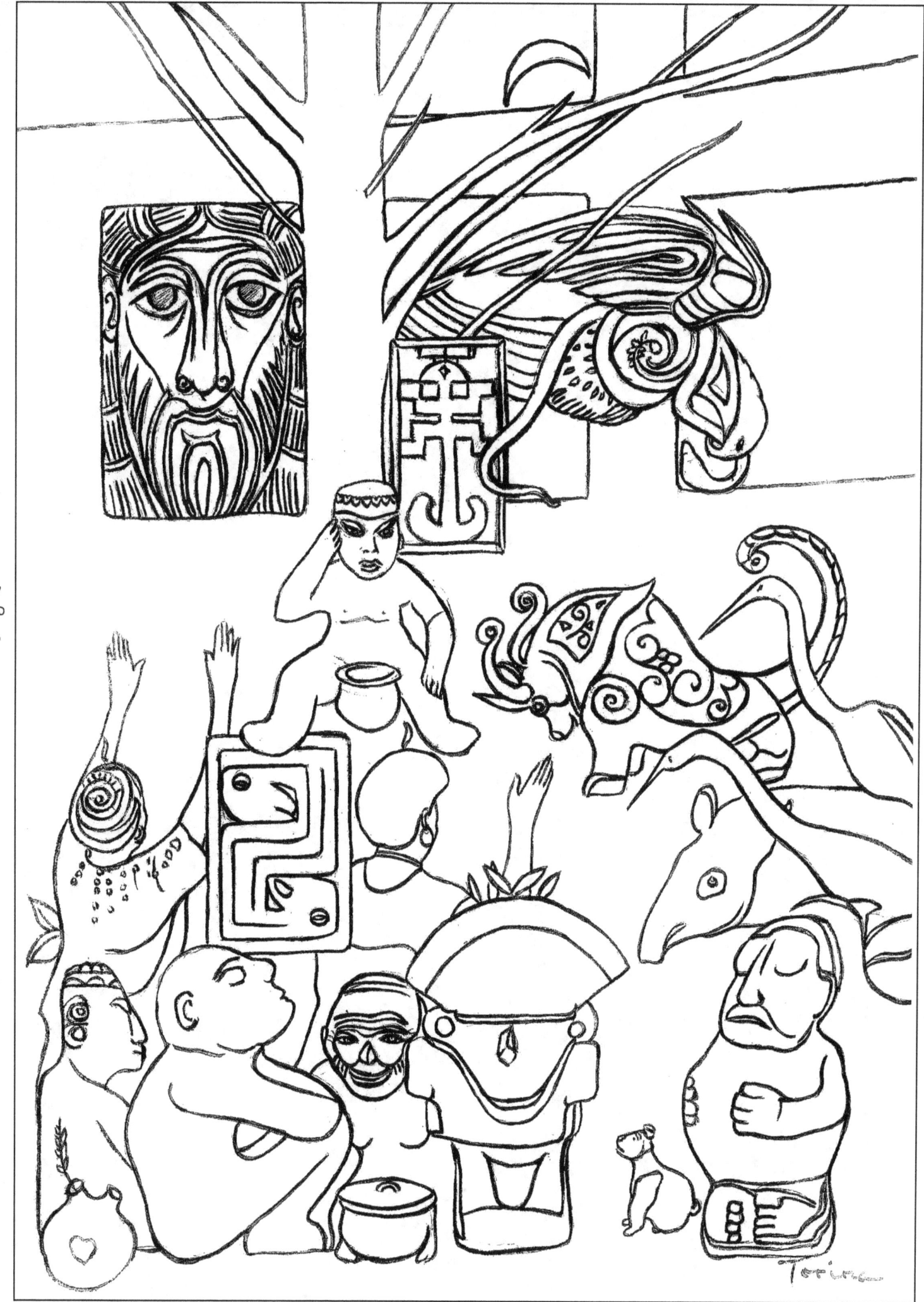

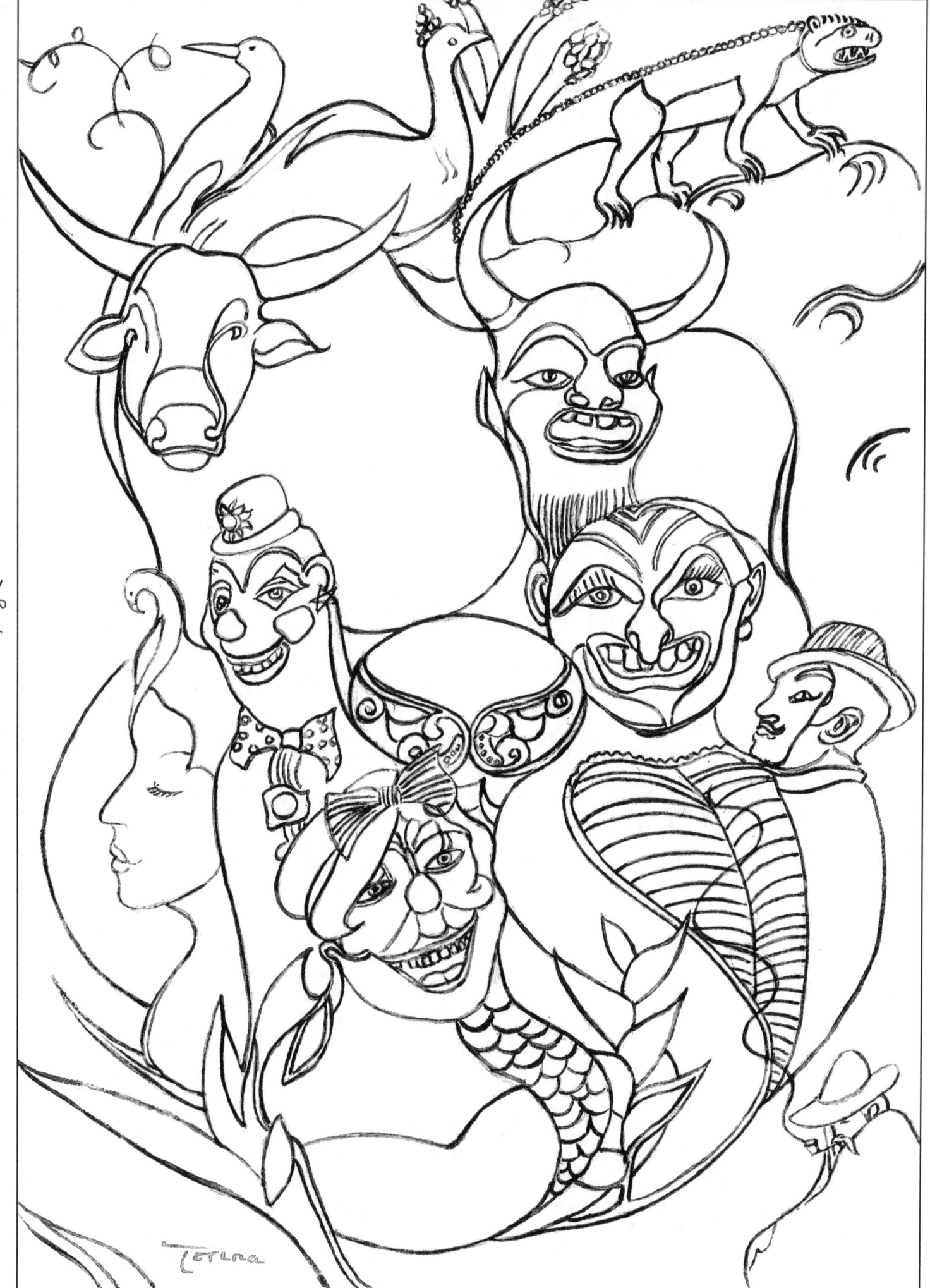

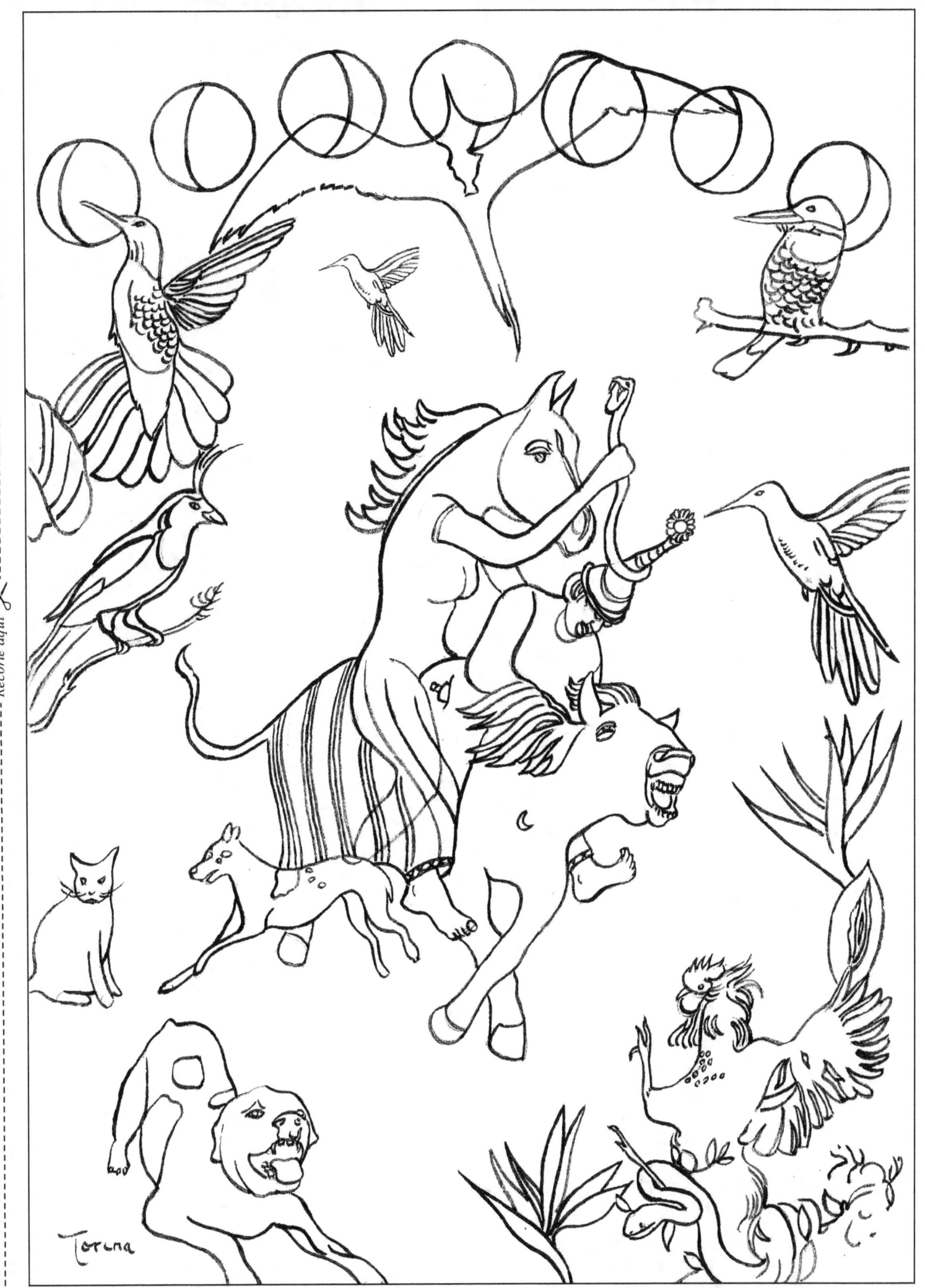

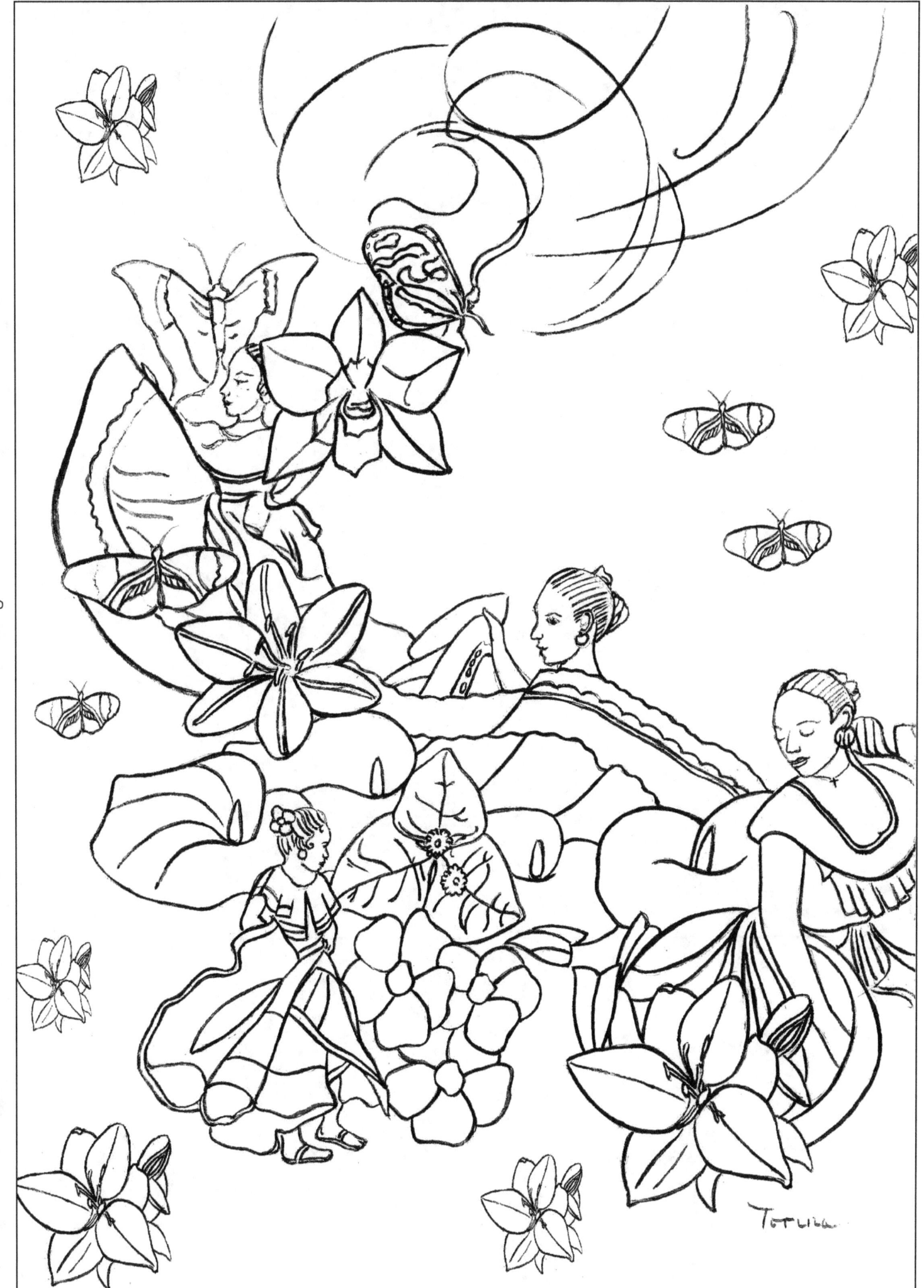

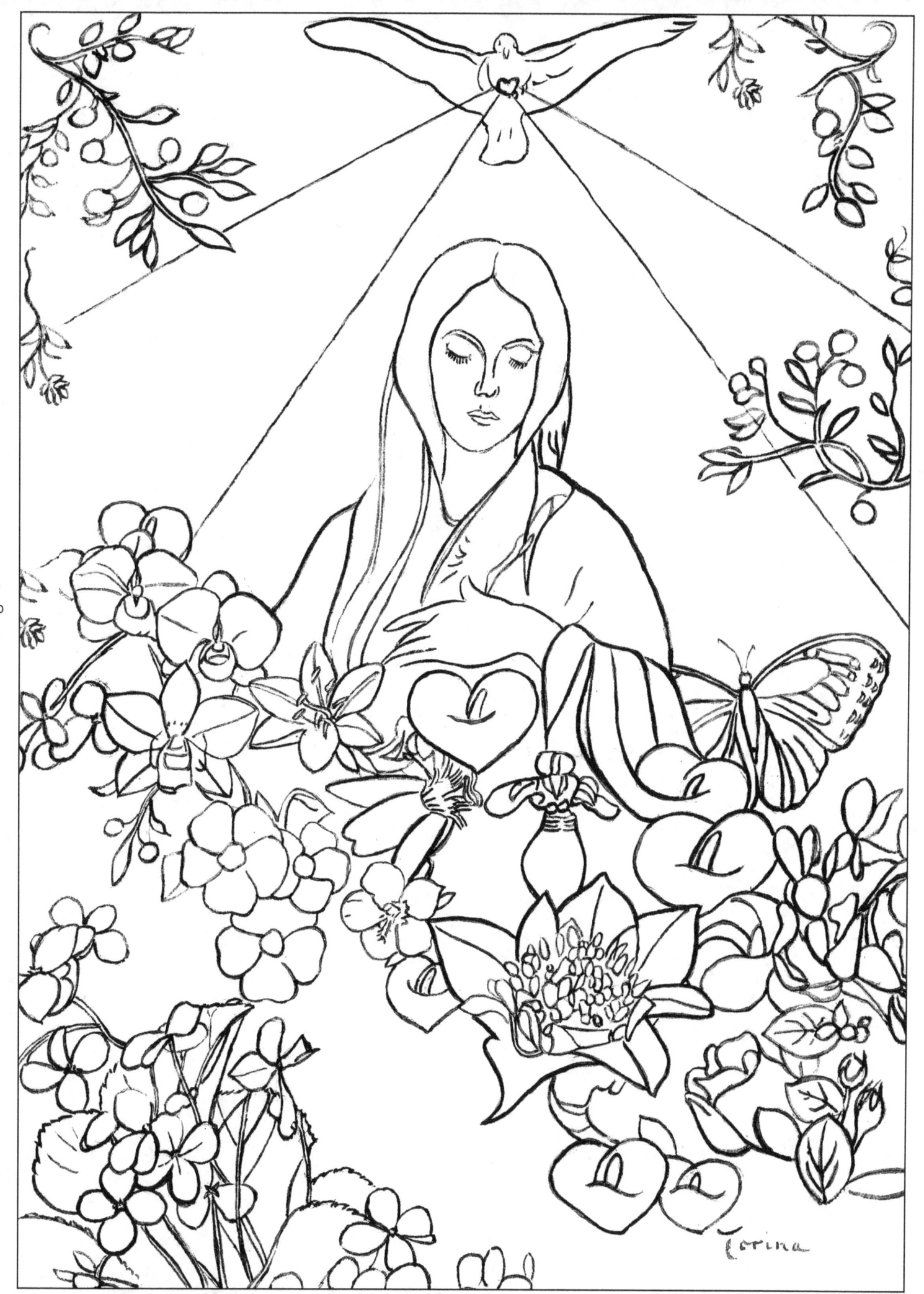

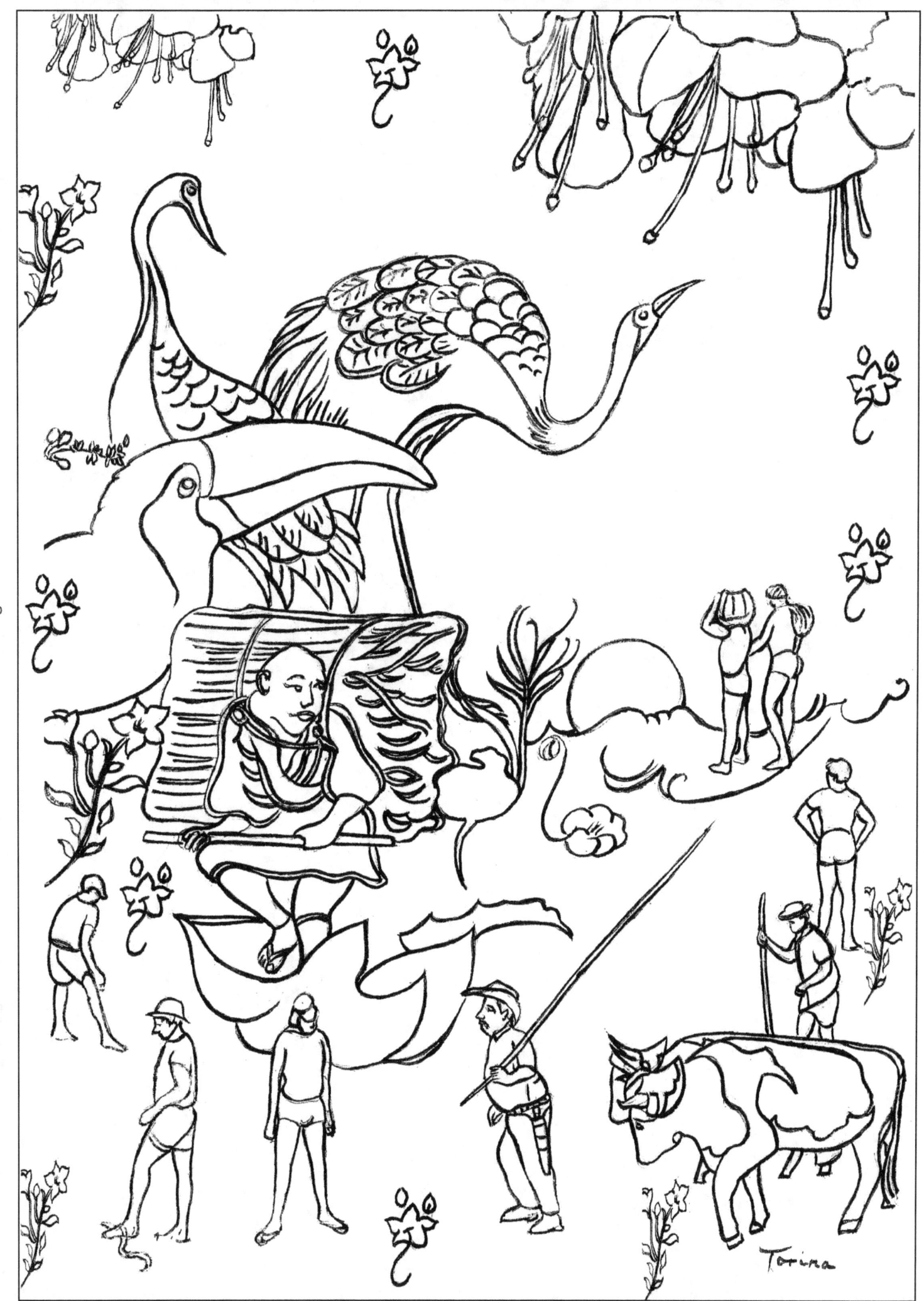

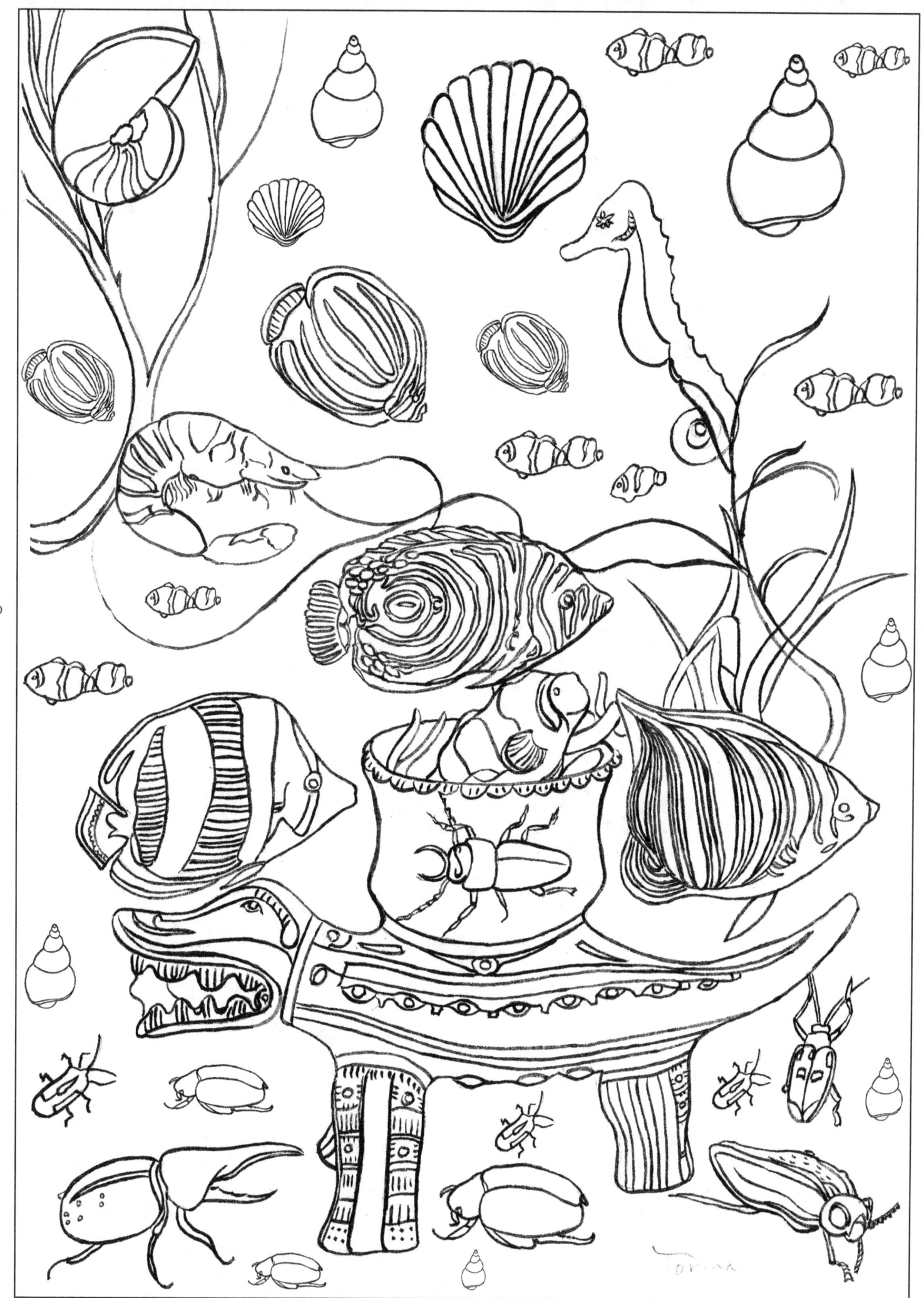

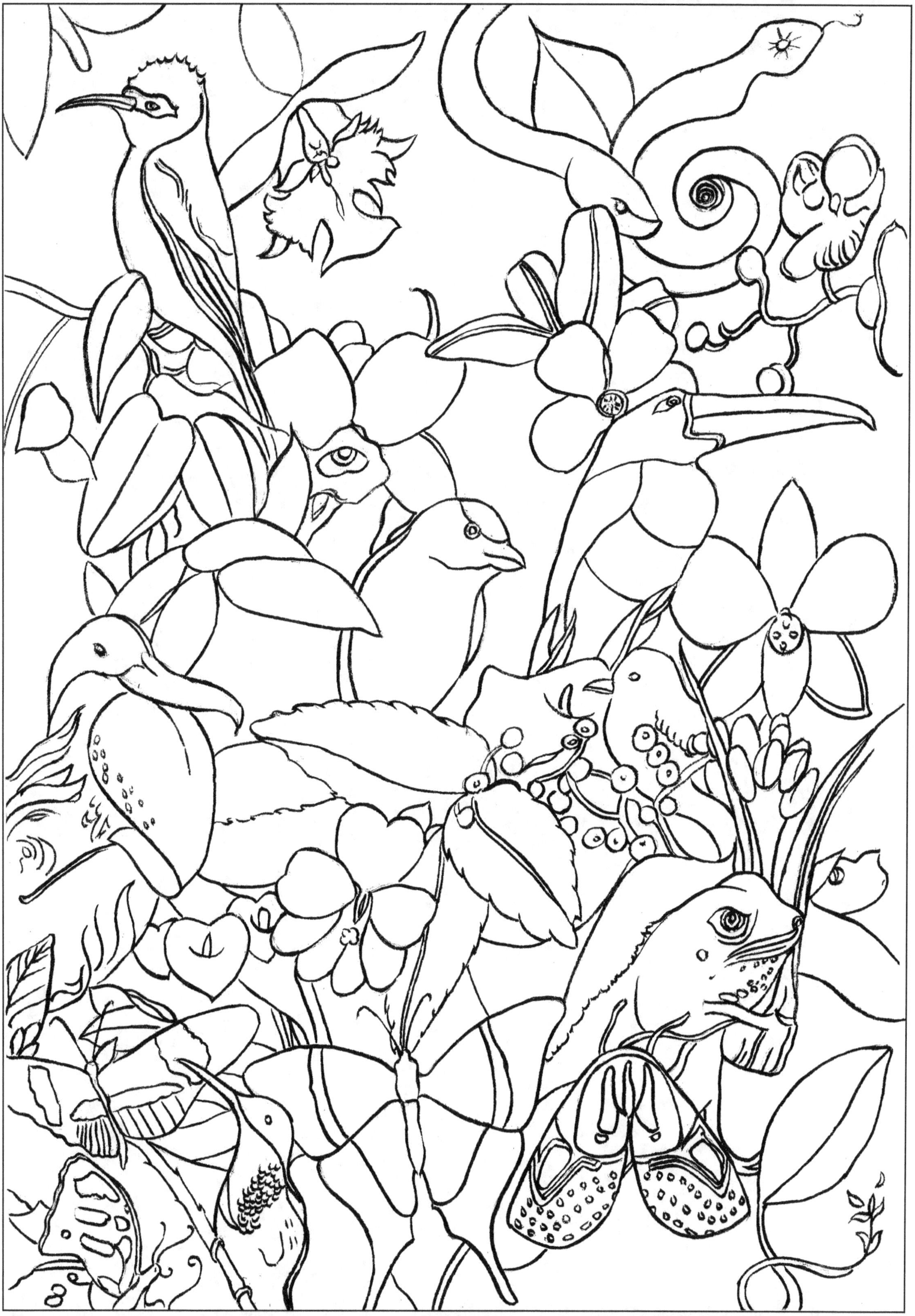

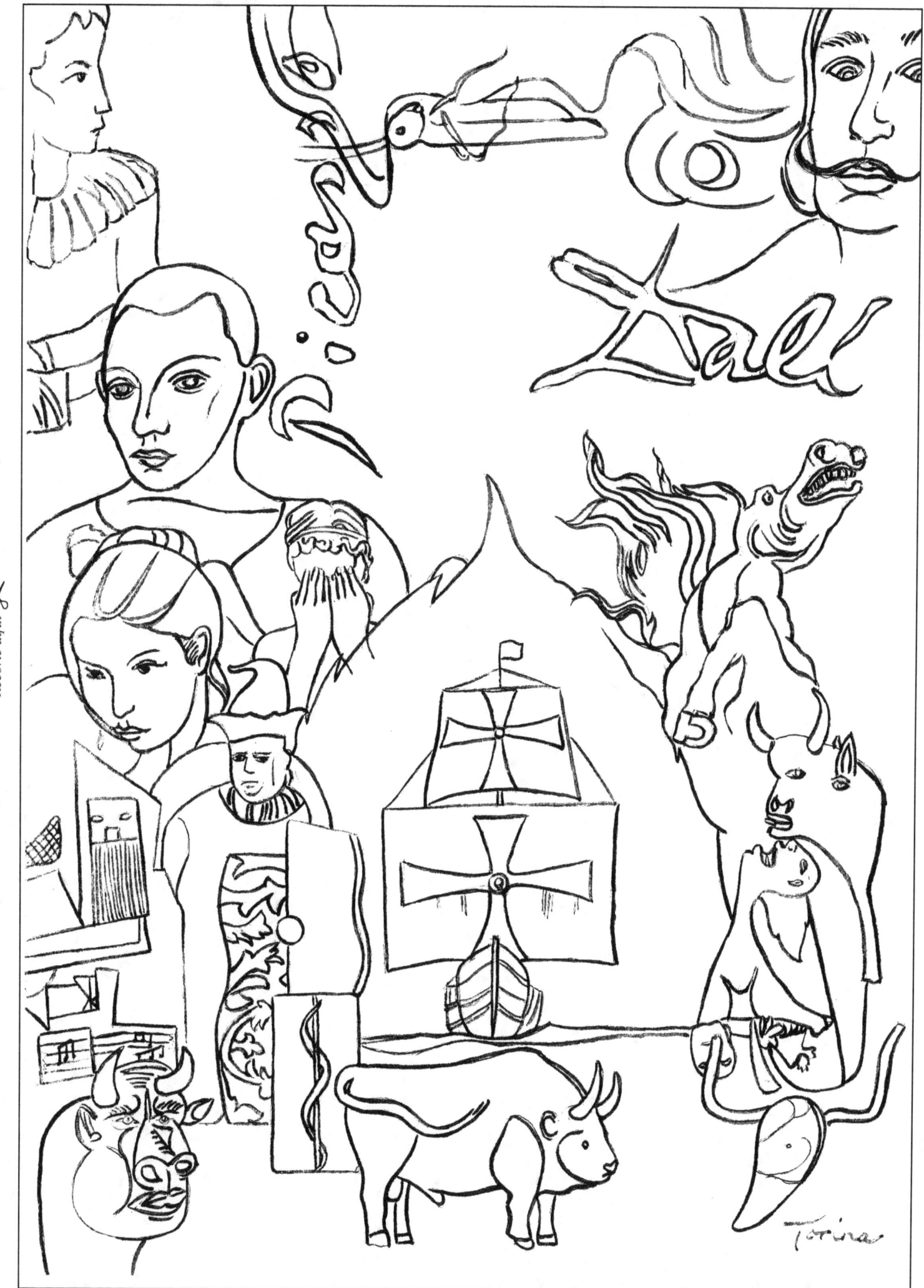

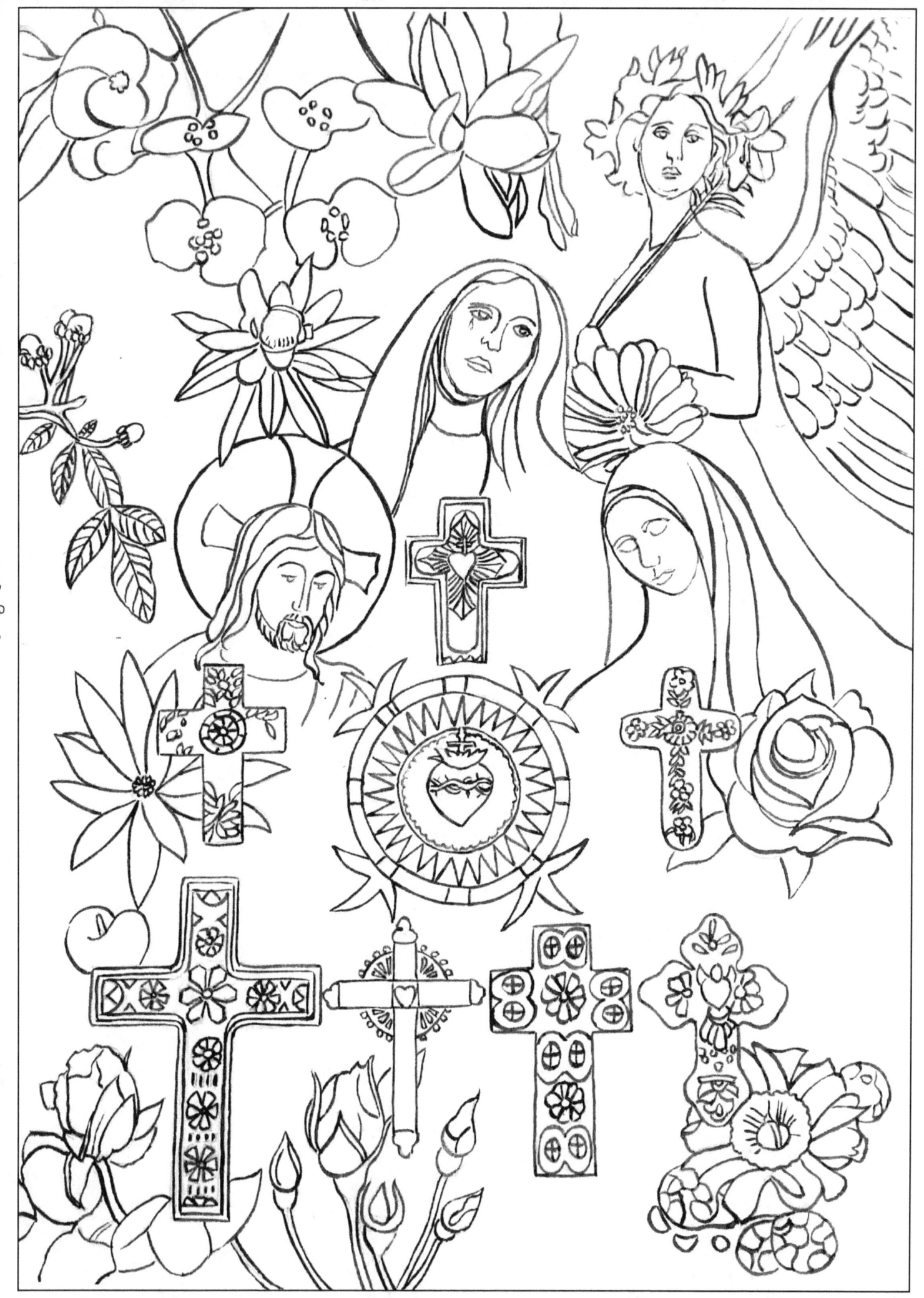

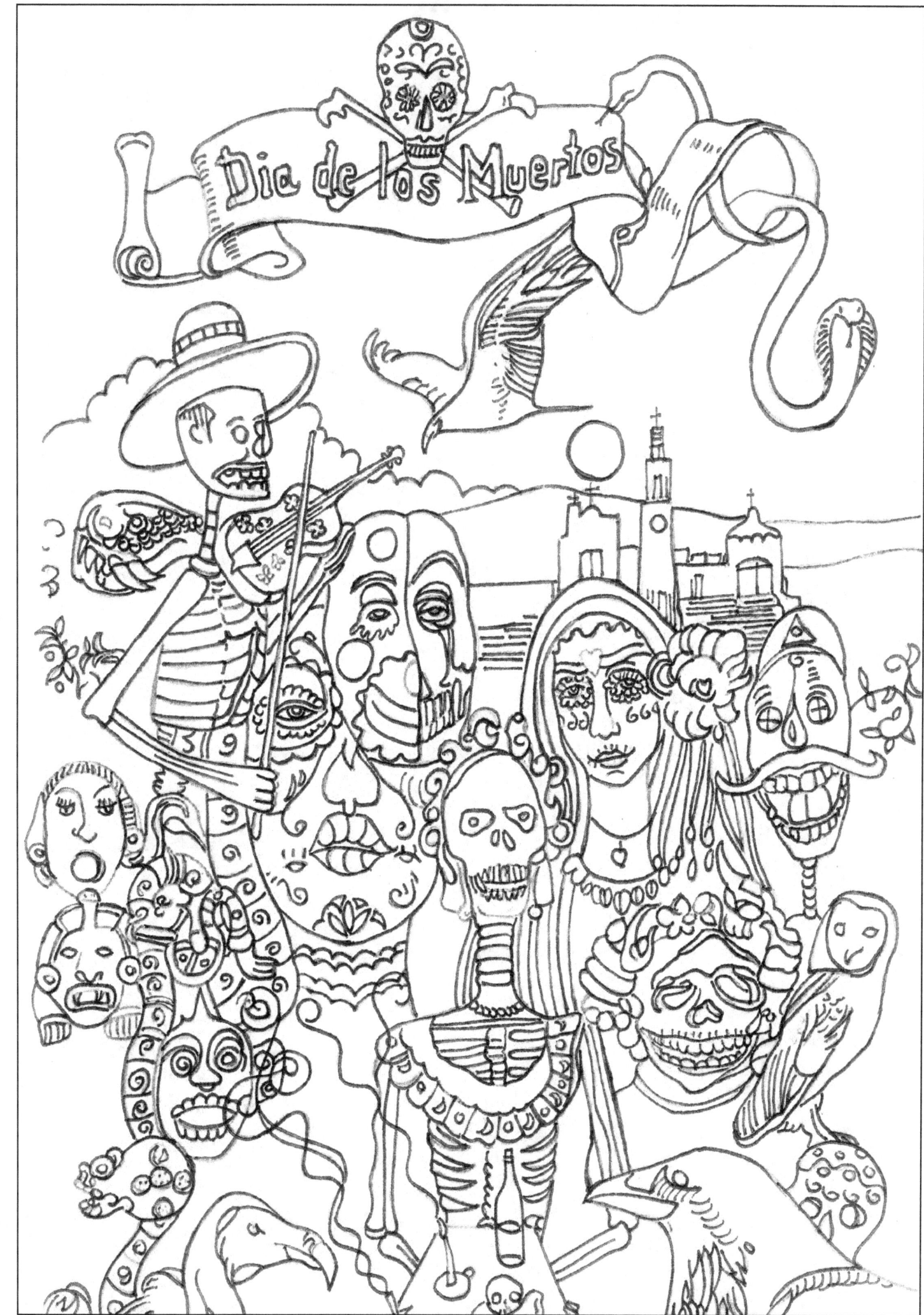

Recorte aquí

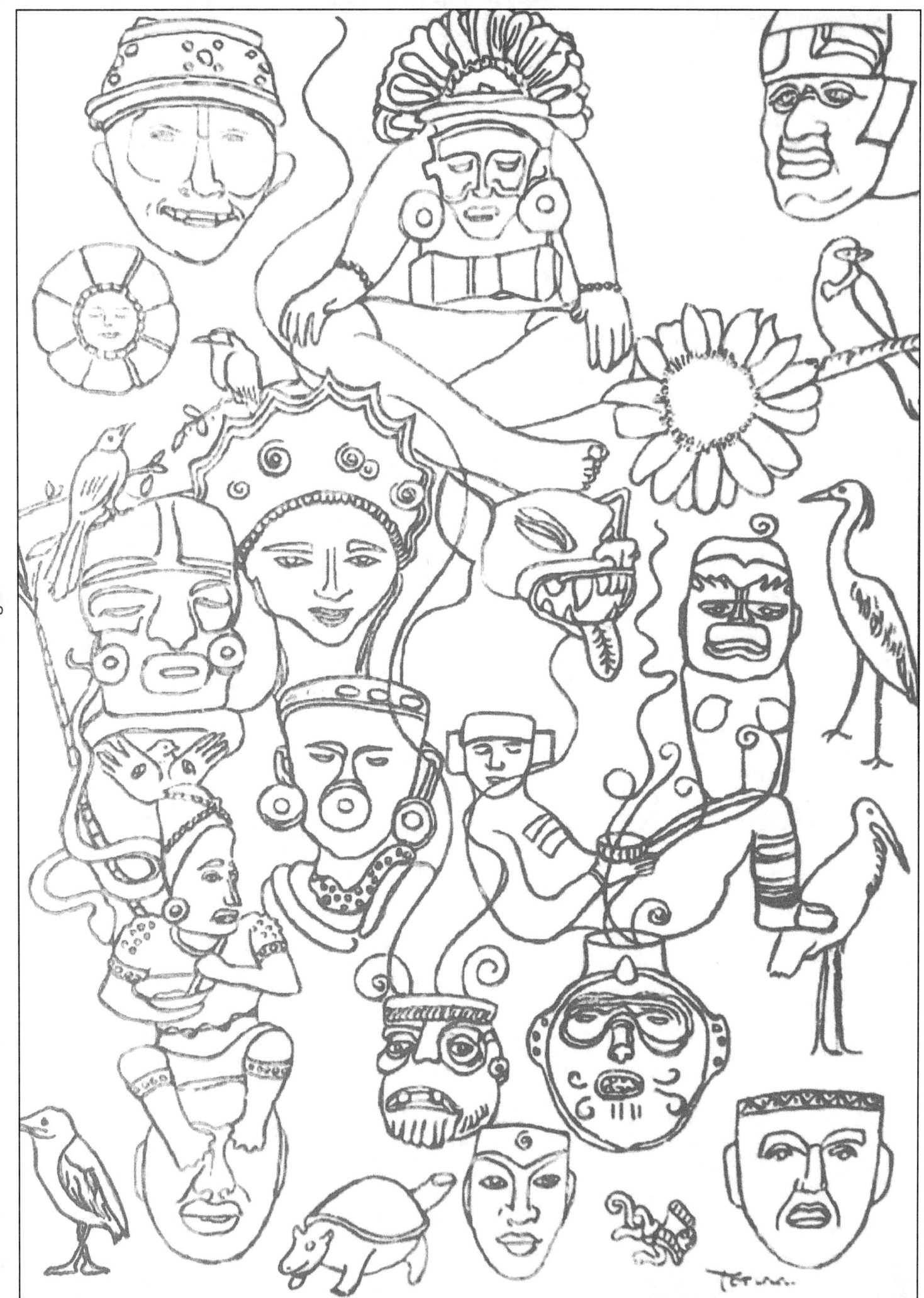

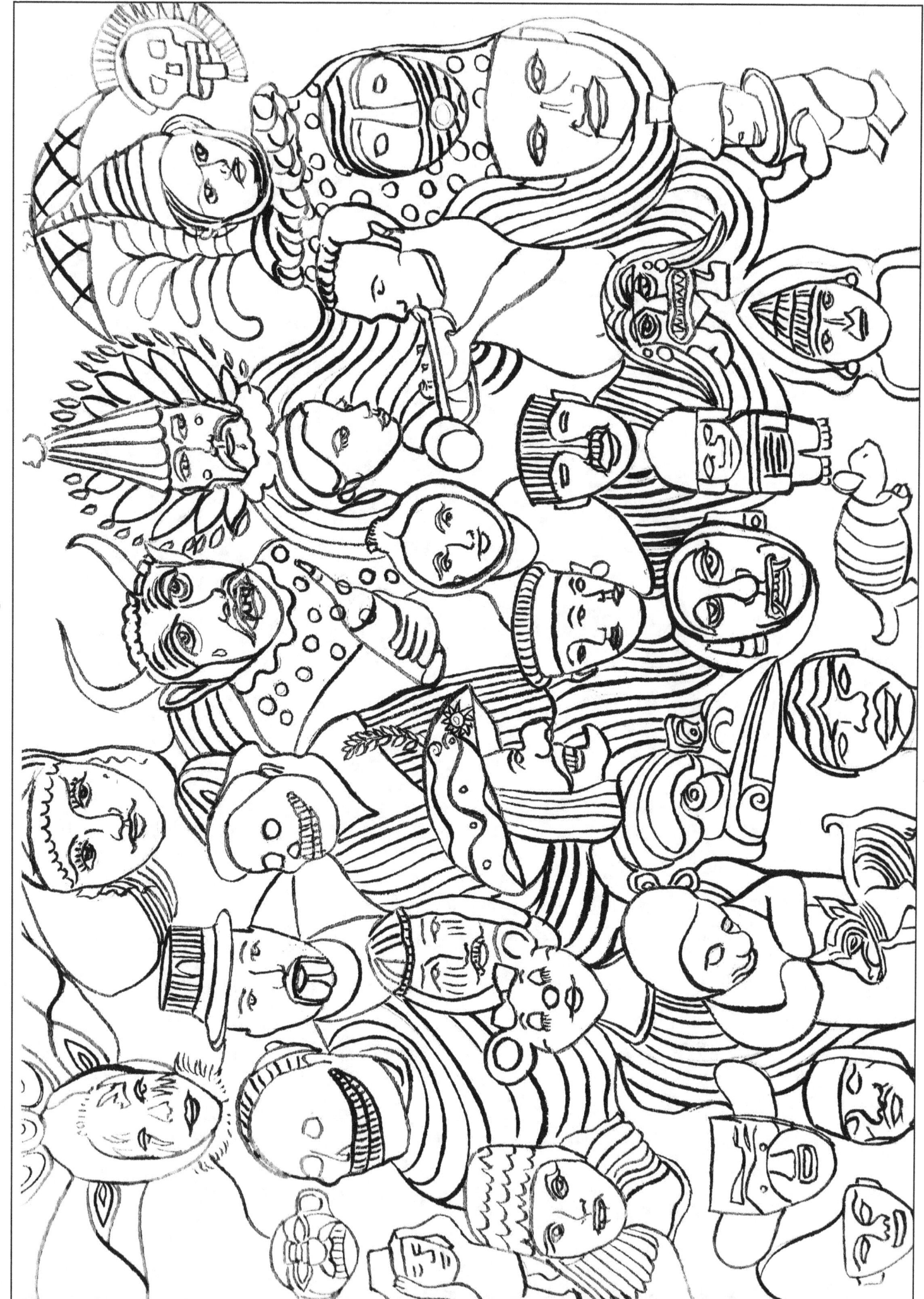

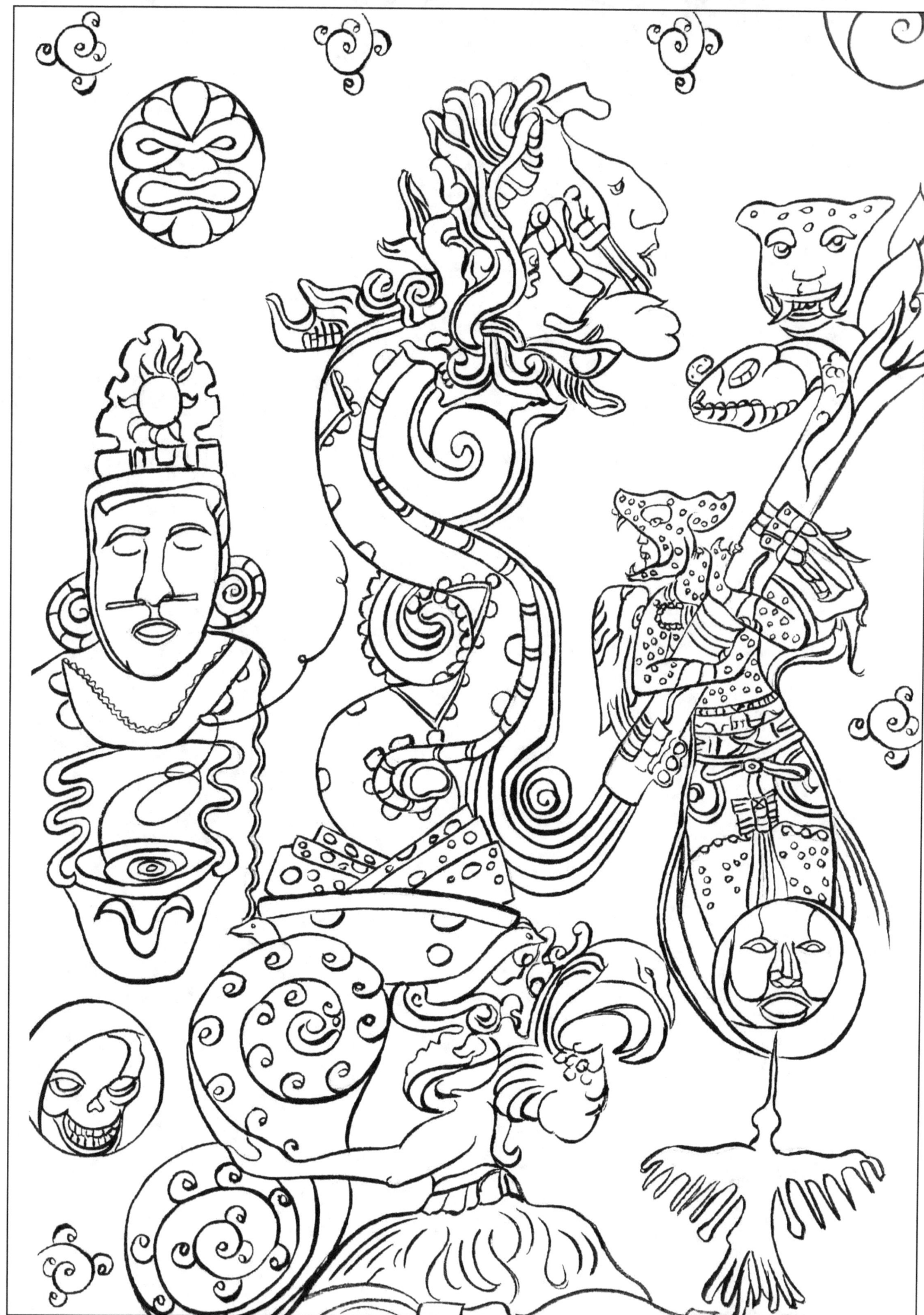

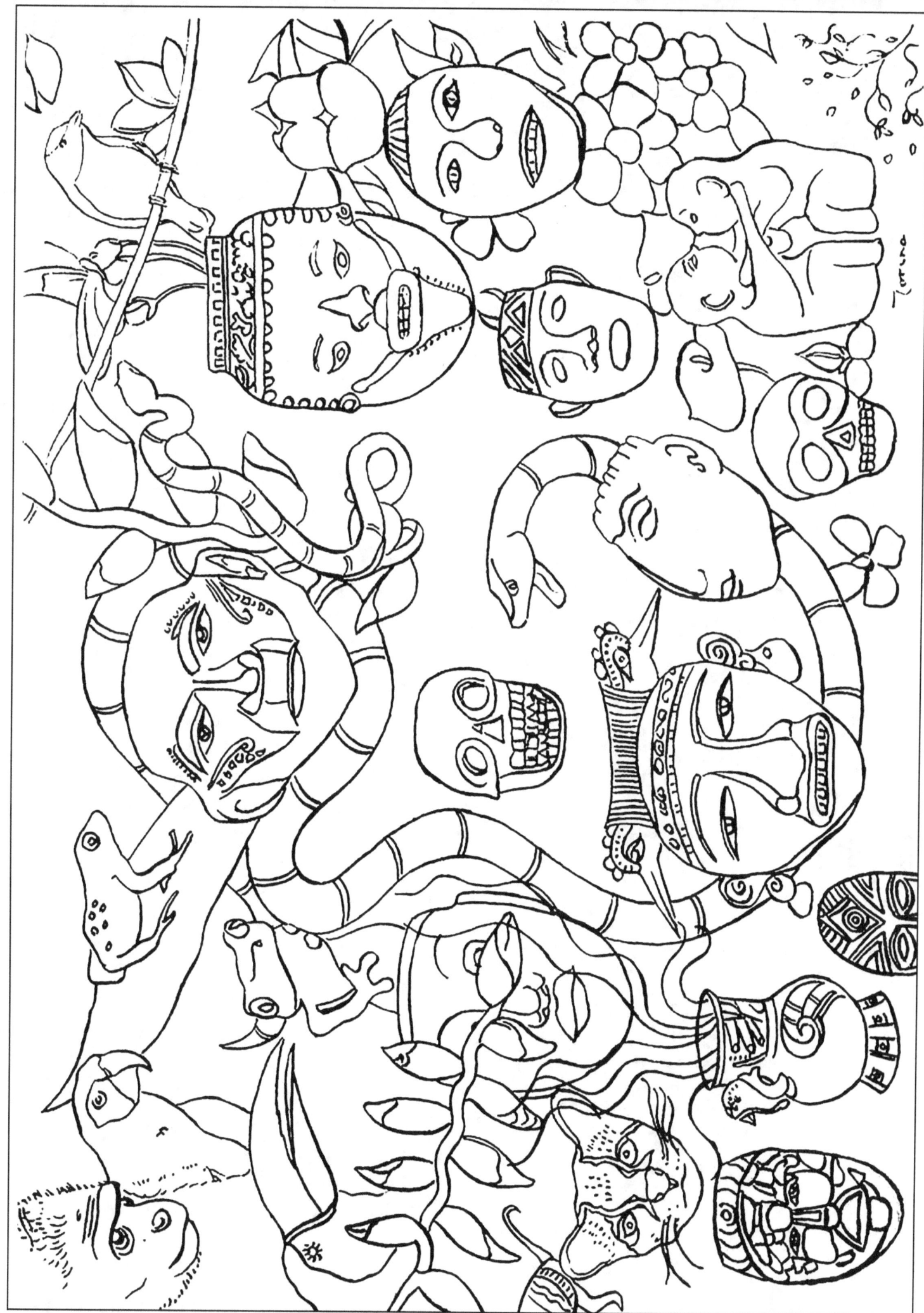

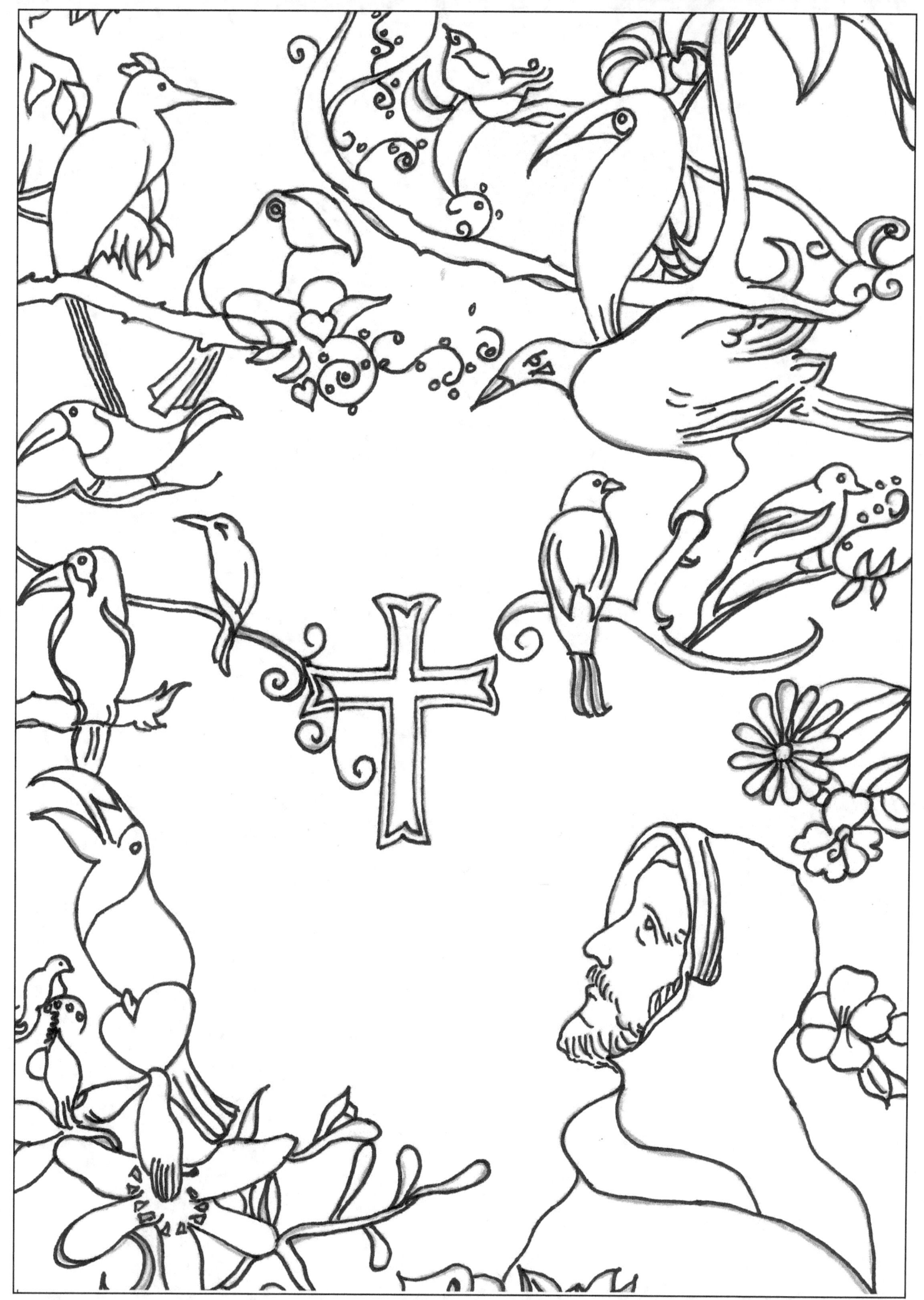

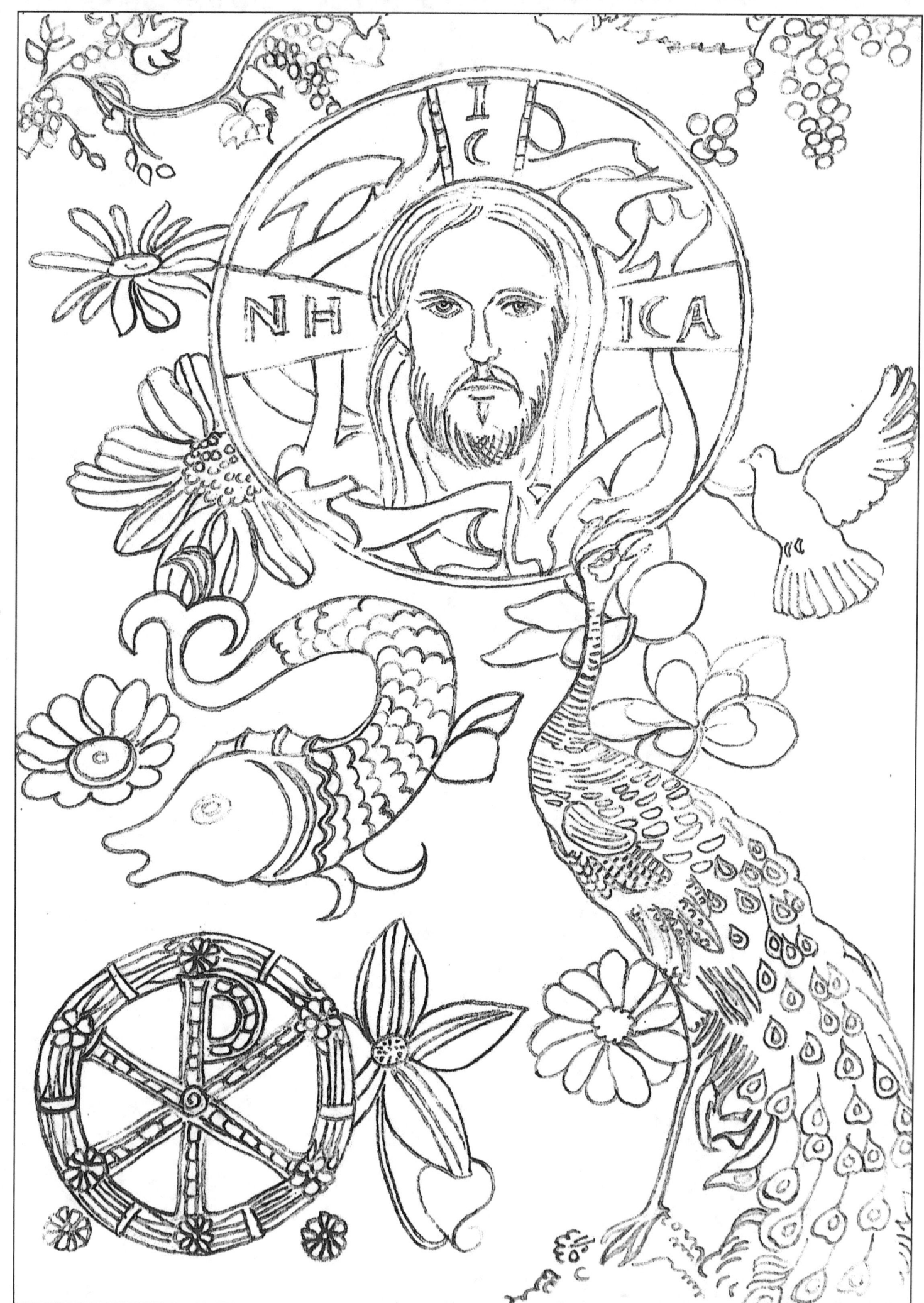

Mardi Gras

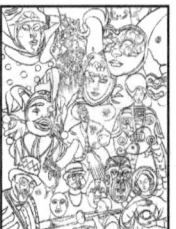

This image was inspired by the famous Mardi Gras festival or Tuesday festival, which annually happens in different cities around the world, 40 days before Palm Sunday according to the Christian calendar. The origin of these celebrations goes back to pagan celebrations of pre-Christian times, corresponding to the rhythm of the seasons and agricultural work.

Buddha

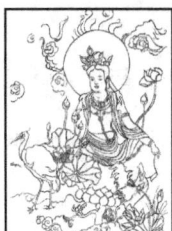

Siddhartha Gautama, known as Gautama Buddha, Sakyamuni, or simply the Buddha, was a sage whose teachings the Buddhism. He born in the extinct Sakia Republic, in the foothills of Himalaya. Buddha is an honorific with religious content that applies to anyone who has achieved full awakening or enlightenment, this awakening involves a state of mental tranquility. This happens after transcend the desire or craving (lobha), aversion (dosha) and confusion (moha).

Art of Ancient Egypt

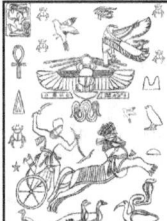

One of the characteristics of ancient Egypt is its singular art, with monumental works that were generally symbolic funeral or religious nature art works. The art form of Egypt continued to inspired thousands of years later. They used to be buried by the desert sand or their owners, to enjoy them in the "afterlife".

Australian Aboriginals

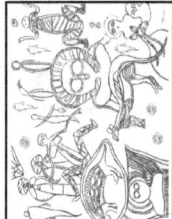

Australian Aboriginal art includes works in a wide range of media, such as painting on leaves, wood carving, stone carving, sculpture, ceremonial clothing and sand painting. They used to paint nature, including animals, lakes and dreaming time, plus stories and legends that were part of their religion.

Peruvian Art

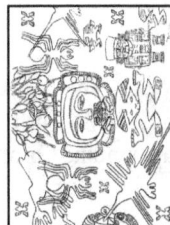

Peruvian art is rooted in Andean societies, located in the Andes Mountains of South America, Peru currently has one of the largest varieties of arts and crafts of the world that over time have been enriched without losing its originality. Art responds to political, social and religious reasons, Peruvian art has responded to its political, social and religious structure and is held in high regard by archeology and its many existing discoveries.

Native American Totems

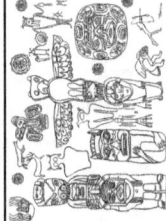

A totem is an object, being or natural animal in the mythologies of some cultures. Is taken as an emblem of the tribe or individual, and may include a variety of attributes and meanings. In some indigenous tribes and native nations, North America's animals reflect supernatural forces and spiritual powers.

African Masks

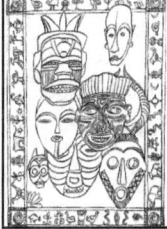

African masks play an important role in traditional ceremonies and dances theater. All African masks fall into one of four categories: the ancestor spirits, mythological heroes, the combination of ancestor and hero, and animal spirits. They are of great importance especially during funeral ceremonies. The mask appoints both, the person who wears the mask and the mask itself. In traditional society, the mask is a religious, political and social institution. It is the mediator between God and the ancestors of men.

Khmer Classical Dance

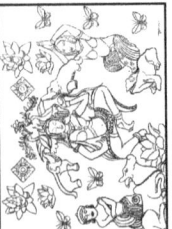

Khmer Classical Dance is a dance of Cambodia that shares some similarities with the classical dances of Thailand and Laos. It is a form of highly stylized art danced mainly by women, Khmer classical dance, during the time of the French protectorate, was limited largely to the courts of the royal palaces, made by the spouses, concubines, relatives and attendants of the palace . Thus, the names for Western art often refer to the royal court.

Chinese Dragon and Cranes

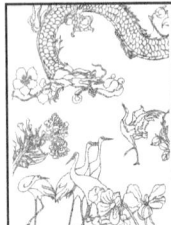

The Chinese dragon is a mythological and legendary animal of China and other Asian cultures that have parts of nine animals: lobster eyes, deer antlers, nose ox, dog nose, whiskers catfish, lion's mane, tail snake, fish scales, claws of an eagle. The dragon is also the embodiment of the concept of yang (male) and is related to time as bringer of rain and water in general. His female counterpart is the Chinese phoenix.

Christmas

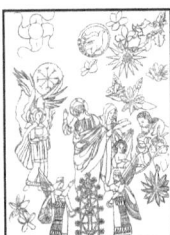

Christmas is one of the most important festivals of Christianity, along with Easter and Pentecost. This feast, which commemorates the birth of Jesus Christ in Bethlehem, is celebrated on 25 December in the Catholic Church, the Anglican Church, some Protestant communities and in most of the Orthodox Churches. It is celebrated on January 7 in other Orthodox Churches and the Russian Orthodox Church or Jerusalem.

Gargoyles

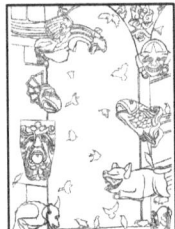

The origin of the gargoyles dates back to the Middle Age and is related to the rise of the bestiary and the torments of hell. In fact, the first gargoyles were baptized with the name of 'taps'. However, the gargoyle iconography is not limited to mere representation of taps, but also embodied other fabulous beings that could take the form of animals, humans or a mix of both; but always represented more or less in a monstrous way.

Women in Kimono

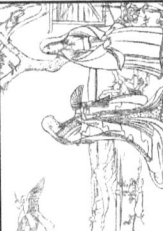

The kimono is the traditional Japanese dress, the garment was commonly used until the early postwar years. The Japanese term mono means "thing" and ki comes from kiru: 'wear, carry'. The cut, color, fabric and decorations vary according to sex, age, marital status, time of year and the occasion. The kimono dress covering the body in surrounding form and fastened with a wide belt called obi.

Etruscans

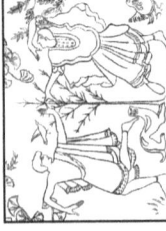

The Etruscans were a people of antiquity whose geographical core was Tuscany, Italy. A predecessor of Rome and heir to the Hellenic world mode, culture (they were outstanding goldsmiths and innovative shipbuilders) and military techniques were superior. In 40 A.C., they lost their political independence. However, the Etruscan presence was always outstanding, the last three kings of Rome were Etruscans.

Graffiti

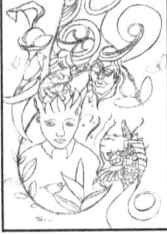

It's called "pintada", or graphite to a form of free painting, noted for its illegality, usually performed in urban spaces. Its origin dates back to the inscriptions on walls have been since the days of the Roman Empire, especially those that are satirical or critical.

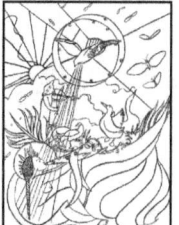

Mother earth touched by Seven Rays

The seven rays are part of a theosophical concept found in some religions and doctrines denoted. Each ray represents a quality by a color, representing and chakra, guided by a star and identifies a kingdom and a jewel. The qualities are represented will and power, love and wisdom, active intelligence, harmony, concrete science, love-devotion and ceremonial order.

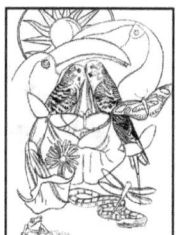

The Garden

With only 0.03% of the global land area, Costa Rica has a huge variety of wildlife, largely due to its geographical position between the continents of North and South America, its neotropical climate and its wide range of habitats. Costa Rica is home to more than 500,000 species, representing nearly 6% of estimated worldwide, making Costa Rica one of the 20 countries with the highest biodiversity in the world's total species.

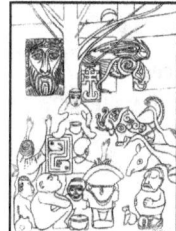

Evolution of Art in Faith

Christian art is created to illustrate and supplement in a tangible way the Christian message. As sacred art, for believers Christian art has as its essential purpose worship. Each piece of Christian art, regardless of the medium, or the character, event, biblical passage (the periscopes, parables) or concept it represents, usually contain identifying symbols of the branch of Christianity that produced it.

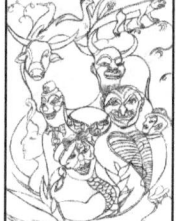

The Masquerade

Traditional Costa Rican Masquerade is a popular tradition of Costa Rica that has roots in the colonial era, and today is still very current. Its origin is the product of colonial and American Indian festive practices. The characters are called "mantudos" or clowns, and are characterized by strolling through the streets during the popular or religious festivals and shifts, chasing attendees dancing to music "cimarrona" and accompanied by fireworks. 1997, October 31 was declared National Day of the Costa Rican Traditional Masquerade.

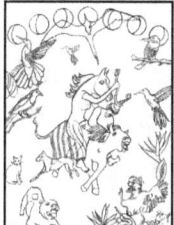

The Segua

The Segua (Nahuatl, cihuatl woman), is a character of a typical legend of Central America, of Mesoamerican origin, and speaks of a spectral being that appears at night passers-by lonely roads in the form of a very beautiful woman, who asks for help to take her to a nearby village. Once the creature has jumped on the horse (or vehicle, in modern versions), it is transformed into a horrifying being with the head of a horse skull with the appearance as if in a state of putrefaction.

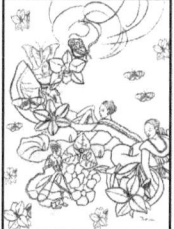

The Punto Guanacasteco

The guanacasteco point or costarican point is a native Costa Rican folk dance of Costa Rica, considered the national dance of the country. The point is a dance of Dominican origin that spread to Cuba, Costa Rica and Panama. Generally, the point has no lyrics, and is accompanied with "bombs", type of verse that is inserted when the music at the request of the dancers is interrupted.

The Virgin Mary

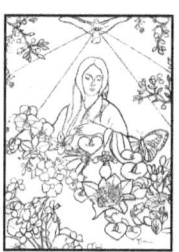

The presence of Mary in Christianity was not a single witness, but of a qualified person and in more than one sense, exclusive participant in a key moment in the history of salvation, the incarnation of Jesus Christ, the crucifixion and death of Jesus, and the formation of the first Christian community praying immediately before the coming of the Holy Spirit at Pentecost. In the Catholic and Orthodox Churches there attributed powers of intercession trough her in that she is the Holy Mother of God.

Labor Day

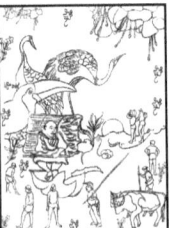

San José Obrero, the carpenter of Nazareth, work remediated the needs of Mary and Jesus. For this reason, on this day, Christian workers honor St. Joseph as a model and their patron. It was after the time of industrialization when the party took shape.

Ocean life

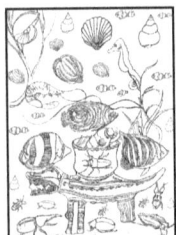

There was an established cultural center that flourished for about 2000 years at the Great Nicoya. Nicoyan society managed to achieve a complex social organization and a high degree of development cultural. A the arrival of the Spanish in the sixteenth century, they found cities and complex governments, specialized agriculture including irrigation, arts and crafts, highlighting the triad polychrome pottery (whose tradition has been inherited by Guanacastecans craftsmen to this day), the production of jade jewelry and manufacturing stone "metate".

The Garden

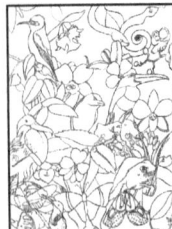

Huge range of colors in their plumage, as well as countless and incredible singing birds make Costa Rica admired by foreign and domestic tourists. In national parks and wilderness areas 900 kinds of species, Costa Rica tops the list of tropical forests, from the altitude of the clouds to humid lowlands of the tropical.

The Conquest

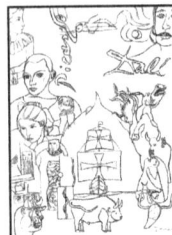

The exploration and conquest of America took place during the so-called age of discovery, which followed the arrival of Christopher Columbus in 1492, from the late fifteenth century and during the sixteenth century. The greatly influencer of Latin America culture was the artistic revolution marked by Salvador Dali and Pablo Picasso.

Reliquaries

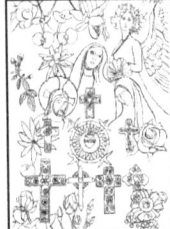

When the Spanish and Portuguese decided to explore and conquer the New World for the Crown and the Church, they took their personal belongings, including devotional items to inspire and comfort them in their travels, such as rosaries, crosses, medals, triptychs, and medallions contain small religious images. In the Americas and the Philippines during the colonial era these shrines evolved a unique genre of devotional jewelry and artistic expression.

Day of the Dead

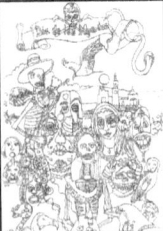

Day of the Dead is greatly celebrated in Mexican and Central American countries, It is of Mesoamerican origin honoring the dead celebration. Mainly it held on 1 and 2 November, coinciding with the Catholic celebrations of All Souls Day and All Saints. The festivities were presided over by the goddess Mictecacíhuatl, known as the "Lady Death" (now related to "La Catrina") and wife of Mictlantecuhtli, Lord of the land of the dead. The festivities were dedicated to the celebration of children and the lives of deceased relatives.

Ancient Mayas

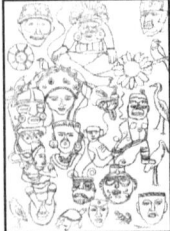

The classic Mayan art is appreciated for its excellent ideas. The carvings and stucco reliefs of Palenque and the statuary of Copan are especially fine and objects reflect rich and diverse society.

Festival de los Locos

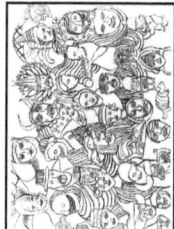

One of the most anticipated events in San Miguel de Allende, in the state of Guanajuato, Mexico, during the year is the traditional Parade of Fools, the first weekend after the day of San Antonio de Padua is celebrated, which is the June 13th of each year. In this festival men dressed as women and women dressed man parade through San Miguel. During the parade participants throw candy to children and spectators.

Quetzalcoátl

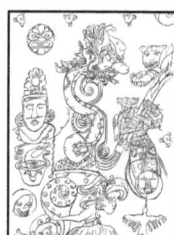

Quetzalcoatl, also considered "The Feathered Serpent", represents the duality inherent in the human condition: the "snake" is physical body with its limitations and "feathers" are the spiritual principles. Another name applied to this deity is Nahualpiltzintli, "prince of nahuales". Quetzalcóatl is also the Nahuatl name of the Mesoamerican Messiah and the title of the supreme priests of the Toltec religion. It manifested itself in various historical prophets, the last of which was Topiltzin Ce Ácatl king of Tula, who lived between the years 895 and 947 of the Christian era.

Jungle

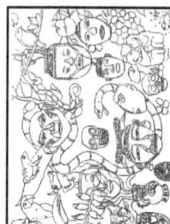

Costa Rica is the country with the greatest biodiversity per square kilometer of territory with 1.8 species per square kilometer. Costa Rica is south of Central America in the inter-tropical zone of the planet. The inter-tropical zones of the Americas are home to more biodiversity than other continents. In the jungle it is common to find tree species such as the yellow almond, sparrow hawks, caobilla, ojoche and is also quite common to observe peccary, agoutis, green macaws and a variety of other bird species characteristics of this type of forest.

Saint Francis of Assisi

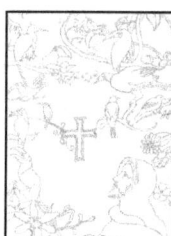

Francis of Assisi was born on October 3, 1226 .. It is an Italian saint, who was a deacon, founder of the Franciscan Order, born under the authority of the Catholic Church in the Middle Ages. Being the son of a wealthy merchant of the city, he went to live in the strictest poverty and observance of gospels. His religious life was austere and simple, so encouraged his followers to do likewise. It is the first known case in the history of visible and external stigmatization. He was canonized by the Catholic Church in 1228, and his feast is celebrated on October 4.

Symbols

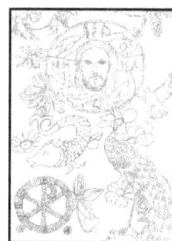

The religious symbolism is the official identification of a religious culture used in rituals. The definition and preservation of the dogmas of faith demanded caution in such a diverse and syncretism as soon as the Roman Empire in those centuries environment. For example to recognize the faithful "insiders" will use symbols. Christian symbolism is a complement of the arcane protects the purity of the faith of external enemies. Turkey and phoenix symbolize the resurrection. Palm victory. The dove Christian simplicity, modesty and peace granted to the faithful soul. Deer, diligent servant of Christ. The anchor, the hope of salvation. The ship, the Church. The fish symbolized "Jesus Christ, Son of God, Savior."